# JAWAHARLAL NEHRU UNIVERSITY NORTH GATE

Harjeet Singh Gill
Professor Emeritus
Jawaharlal Nehru University

**First Published 2021**

ISBN 978–93–83723–74–4



*Published by*
**LG PUBLISHERS DISTRIBUTORS**
49, Street No. 14, Pratap Nagar,
Mayur Vihar Phase I, Delhi 110091
lgpdist@gmail.com

*Printed at*
Sapra Brothers, Noida

for my grand-daughter

Jaspal

president of Union Nationale des Etudiants de France

## IN THE FOLLOWING PAGES

A FLICKER OF LIGHT IN THE DARK NIGHT

JNU NORTH GATE

STAY HOME, GO HOME

THINKING AND COGNITION

THE MAY SIXTY-EIGHT MOVEMENT

THE TRIAL OF JOAN OF ARC

# A FLICKER OF LIGHT IN THE DARK NIGHT

She was a flicker of light in the dark night. We met fifty years ago in our student days in Paris. On the birth of our first child, the daughter, Sandrine, she wrote a poem, Lucioles, Jugnu, who flicker in the dark nights of Sawan. Our frequent visits to Leh sort of converted her to Buddhism. She translated Japji and Jap Sahib into French, also a number of other classical texts of Punjabi language and culture. Some of them were published along with my writings. Others are preserved in a manuscript, Echos du pays des cinq rivières, Echos of the country of five rivers. Sandrine became Chief of a Section in the Archaeological Survey of France. The other two children, Eric and Anila, continued with their academic careers.

There are so many myths about the lucioles. In yonder days, in the now forgotten and almost lost past, there were no electric lamps, not even earthen ones. So, it appears, the artists and the writers used to have these jugnus in transparent vases. It is in the paisible sight of these beautiful creatures and their soothing light that some of the master pieces of the ancient world were composed. When the evening dawned, when the scorching heat and the burning light of the sun faded away, the scribes, the philosophers sat down under the flickering light of these marvellous creatures, and far from the madding crowd, meditated and reflected upon the affairs of this world, the world that was not always very sympathetic and gentle, and discerned and articulated the wisdom of the cosmic universe. Even our grand-mothers and great-grand-mothers sought their light to wind up the small chores of the day.

After a few years in India, in Patiala, she wrote a doctoral thesis on the Phrase Structure of Punjabi for the University of Sorbonne, Paris, and continued to teach there. The family was physically separated, between Paris and JNU, but like the flickers of the jugnus, there were frequent reunions with travels throughout the length and breadth of Bharat. The night was always dark but there were flickers of light with new adventurous ideas and thoughts in our intellectual pursuits.

So it continued for fifty long years in this mundane world of strife and struggle, of jealousies and friendships, of faiths and betrayals. And in the evening of April 23, the luciole, Danielle Gill, had her last flicker at her home in Paris, a home which was once visited by a number of highly distinguished academicians of France.

THE TRIBUNE, April 28, 2020.

# JAWAHARLAL NEHRU UNIVERSITY NORTH GATE

The North Gate of Jawaharlal Nehru University is shut. There are barricades all over. The police vans are moving in and out side of the vast and wild campus without finding their way in any direction. There are nil gais, peacocks, jackals, foxes and serpents. There are also students and professors discussing and debating surrealistic, intellectual and political ideas in class rooms, hostels and dhabas. The North Gate is shut... There is NO Exit.

There is nothing new as far as JNU is concerned. The university has seen worse days. However, this time, it is very different. The upheavals in JNU in January 2020 shook the entire country. The institutions of higher learning all over joined the chorus. The police of the political masters did not spare any student, a girl or a boy, any teacher, a woman or a man. All were handled with equal brutality. The wild fire spread to Jamia, to Aligarh, to Delhi U, to Banaras Hindu U, to Bombay, to Jadavpur, to practically every IIT, to the Science Institute of Bangaluru, to innumerable institutes of higher learning all over Bharat. These university campuses were supposed to be the temples of knowledge. Temples of Knowledge, yes, but certainly not the temples of Devotion and Worship.

The students studied the six schools of ancient India, the Mimansa, the Vaidanta, the Samkhyas, the Yoga, the Nyaya Vaishishika. The great grammarians, Panini, Bhartrihari, and of course, the great linguist philosophers of Buddhism, Nagarjun, Dignaga and Dharmakirti. But they did not stop there.

They were students of all traditions, Indian and others. They studied the great Muslim philosophers, Kindi, Farabi, Averroes who had translated Plato and Aristotle into Arabic and had interpreted their sacred texts in terms of logic and reason acquired from the Greek texts. It was this knowledge of Greek thought that was later reintroduced in Europe, for these texts were lost in the Latin world, that became the bedrock of renaissance in Europe.

The students also studied the modern thinkers, Descartes and Spinoza, Hegel and Marx, Sartre and Lévi-Strauss, Merleau-Ponty and Althusser, Lacan and Foucault, and so on. They lived in a universe of ideas. Nothing was foreign to them. This was the world far beyond the horizons of the communal fundamentalists, of the Khap Panchayats. They rose in unison, irrespective of their religious or linguistic back grounds, they transcended the narrow definitions of state and nation. And, it was so universal, the students and teachers of all Indian institutes of higher learning shook the entire political set up.

I have included here two more papers written earlier on May 68 Students Movement in France and The Trial of Joan of Arc.

The North Gate of Jawaharlal Nehru University is shut. There are barricades all over. The police vans are moving in and out side of the vast and wild campus. There are nil gais, jackals and serpents. There are also students and professors charged with extraordinary intellectual and political ideas discussing and debating in class rooms, hostels and dhabas...There is No Exit.

Harjeet Singh Gill
Professor Emeritus
Jawaharlal Nehru University

*The Students and the Teachers of the world unite. You have nothing to lose but ignorance and fanaticism.*

Jawaharlal Nehru University is a vast campus. From Munirka to Vasant Kunj, it covers several thousand acres of green and pure air. It is a wild campus. There are unbridled intellectuals who indulge in the most surrealistic ideas of church and state. There are wild animals, nil gais, peacocks, jackals, foxes, serpents. Both live in perfect harmony.

The wild intellectuals, students and teachers, play with the ideas from all corners of the earth, from all philosophical and scientific traditions. Nothing is foreign to the seekers after truth, wherever it may be, from whosoever it may be. There are contradictions, contrasting opinions, even amongst the great of the greatest thinkers. Panini was a great grammarian. So was Bhartrihari. For Panini, a grammatical construct, a word, was the ultimate unit. No, said Bahrtrihari, a word has no significance of its own. It is the *sphota*, the utterance, the signifying unit, that matters, the words are simply a part within, which acquire their signification from the way they are constituted within the *sphota*. It was a complete reversal of the Paninian grammar. The Buddhist grammarian philosophers, especially Dignag and Dharmakirti went further and challenged Bhartrihari on the natural and the conventional signification of words. For Bhartrihari, the significance of the linguistic words was natural, fixed for all times. For the Buddhist thinkers, nothing is fixed. Everything is in flux. The words derive their significance from the way they are constituted within a semantic context of the discourse. The Buddhist *Apoha* is a theory of Discourse. Every text, however sacred it may be, is subject to interpretation, an interpretation different from all previous interpretations. The differences between the six schools of Hinduism are well known. For Mimamsa and Vedanta, the Spirit is eternal. For Samkhya and its associates, Yoga, Nayaya Vaishishika, it is Matter that is eternal.

In all religions, there have been divisions, sects, charged with a variety of interpretations that by themselves become classic. Plato, and his student, Aristotle, differed radically on the theory of universals. Against Plato's realism, we have Aristotle's nominalism. These two theoretical views present the western tradition as two poles within which all discussion, all dialogue takes place throughout the centuries. It is often stated that the western philosophical tradition is nothing but foot notes to these two great thinkers of antiquity. One of the greatest Christian philosopher of the fourth century, Saint Augustine, was influenced by neo-Platonic ideas of his time.

When the Europeans had lost the classical Greek texts, Plato and Aristotle were translated into Arabic. In the philosophical fermentation of the ninth century, the great Muslim scholars, Farabi, Kindi, Averroes argued with each other in terms of Aristotelian or Platonic ideas of truth and reality. These debates were later transmitted to the western world that led to the famous European renaissance.

In the nineteenth century, the German thinkers, Hegel to, Marx...were dominant. The twentieth century belongs to the French thinkers, from Sartre to Lévi-Strauss with several other scholars of structuralism and semiotics, Merleau-Ponty, Michel Foucault, Jacques Lacan, Louis Althusser, Lucien Goldman, Roland Barthes, and a number of others. Even earlier, the seventeenth and eighteenth centuries were led by Descartes, Voltaire, Rousseau, the Encyclopaedists, the activists of the French Revolution. The students of JNU have inherited the ideas of all these thinkers.

There are always several conflicting ideologies. Even within a given tradition, there are numerous deviations. I have lectured on Marxism for years. I introduced the major thinkers in this tradition, from Marx to Mao, from Lukacs to Sartre, from Gramsci to Althusser to Lucien Goldman and a host of others. They were all Marxists but they had interpreted Marxism in ways very different from each other. A teacher must discuss all theoretical differences within a given tradition. The students must get used to differences within and without each school of thought. No religion, no ideology is hermetically sealed. The world of ideas is an open-end world. It cannot be shut and closed at the whim of the political leaders.

From following their lectures and reading their basic texts, I realised that not only different thinkers had different ideas but their very expression, their language, their style, their register was different. This is why their translations in English are generally misleading. When I lectured on Sartre or Foucault or Althusser, a number of students from other Centres of social sciences used to attend my lectures. Interestingly, at times, the chairpersons, who themselves considered specialists in the field, refused to sign cards of permission to attend lectures in another Centre even though in JNU this is the rule. A student can follow twenty-five percent courses in any Centre of the university. The chairpersons could not refuse for long because it was the right of the students and they insisted on listening to me. The other professors were reading these texts in English translations that the students had already read. JNU is a university where the students and teachers follow their own intellectual pursuits.

After years of wilderness, first in the United States, then in France, I landed up at Punjabi University, Patiala, as a Professor of Linguistics, in 1968. Just after May 68, it was an interesting experience. Punjab was burning. The Naxalite movement had captured the university space. I met with young activists, most of them had master's degree in English. I personally followed Sartrean tradition, to be a fellow traveller only, never a member of any party. All political parties, like religions, have their infightings, contradictions, conspiracies.

All the same, it was a very refreshing experience. It was a nice homecoming after ten years of intellectual exile. I attended a number of Sahit Sabha conferences where it was invigorating to listen to revolutionary Marxist papers by school and college teachers in chaste Punjabi. They were ideologically lucid. Their articulations demonstrated their understanding and their sincerity. I made some friends who lasted for a number of years. Some of my students in the Department of Anthropological Linguistics, that I founded, worked on Punjabi folk art and culture, some did very incisive analyses of texts written in Punjabi, Urdu and English.

In 1984, I was invited to a Chair in Linguistics in the Centre for Linguistics and English of Jawaharlal Nehru University. JNU was a world apart. Nothing like this could be imagined in India. For me, it represented the best of East and West, of India and Europe. The intellectual atmosphere was humming with ideas from all corners of the globe. The most brilliant students from all over India, from Kashmir to Kanyakumari, from Nagaland to Gujarat, with all possible backgrounds of religion, culture and language were there. They had shed all baggage of their physical space of origin. Saturated with ideas from East and West, of the most avant-garde free thinkers, they had already transcended all national and communal boundaries. There was no question of teaching them anything. In fact, I do not like the concept of 'teaching', it was 'sharing' my knowledge and my intellectual experiences with my young friends. It was just wonderful.

In France, I had married a French girl who taught me French. We often talk about mother tongue. I wonder what is more important, mother tongue or the tongue of your girl-friend? I was soon proficient in French, could follow the extremely complex discourses of the great masters of yonder days. They differed with each other, at times, very passionate debates between Sartre and Lévi-Strauss, between Sartre and Foucault or Althusser. It was also the atmosphere heavily weighed down by the Vietnamese war. I used to attend small revolutionary groups that helped me in making new friends, but more than that, I learned there, the French language which is never found in the books of the savants. Later on, with my own French children, I learnt the French baby talk, called, pipi kaka. All this helped me follow some of the intricacies of the French language of the great thinkers, for, when even the great writers articulate in very pedantic language, there are always expressions which are drawn from the most colloquial register. When her deputation in India was over, my wife and children settled in Paris, I had all the time to study and be with my students. Of course, the contact with Paris continued. We commuted practically every summer in one direction or the other.

After the endless class lectures, the students were welcome to come to my home any time and spend hours discussing what can never be discussed in a class. The atmosphere was just perfect for a wild intellectual life. Then there were parties for one excuse or another. After every viva or seminar, the students and teachers were invited for Rum and Pakora parties at 1313 Poorvanchal. Pakora, I believe, is one of the most important invention of ancient India. Its content can be any variety of veg or non-veg. Its only competitor is samosa but samosa is a later development, hence less important. The wild intellectual fiesta was a permanent feature of JNU life. Our students belonged to all classes and creeds. There were friendships of every possible combination of religion and language which at times turned into regular partnerships. Obviously, these transgressions could not be imagined or accepted by the followers of the Khap Panchayats or the adherents of RSS.

This university order of absolute freedom of thought and action could not be tolerated by the political powers of ignorance and fanaticism. This had to be stopped. They sent an administrator who had never been in any university, who had absolutely no idea of the unique intellectual experience of JNU. He was nominated on the recommendation of the most uneducated minister of education. His creed is fascism. His only mission is to destroy the academic conventions and traditions of JNU. He has done absolutely nothing for the study of Indology, so dear to RSS, in the university. It is not RSS, for even in RSS there are several intelligent and humane persons. I have friends in RSS who are brilliant scholars, who ridicule the test-tube theories of the ignorant, fanatic followers. Like a seasonal blind man he sees nothing but red everywhere. The former education minister, himself a senior BJP leader, admonished him and asked him to quit, but such an advice has had no effect on his stubborn skin. He does not recognise the duly elected representatives of the students. His own government talks to them, accepts most of their demands, but for him, they simply do not exist. All over the world, the university walls are decorated with political posters. He got all the beautiful posters of left and right removed. Now with barren walls, the university looks like a biscuit factory.

In JNU, my experience is not unique. Every other professor has had a very similar intellectual career. The differences only added to the variety and excellence of dialogue and discussion. We all differed with each other. We all respected the right to free thinking and free living. So did the students.

Now suddenly, it is all abhorred. The students and teachers of JNU are considered “anti-national”, for they do not adhere to the dreams and desires of the communal and fundamentalist forces who have acquired political power. In popular democracy, populism works. Communal propaganda is very efficient. After Indira Gandhi was assassinated for her attack on the Golden Temple, three thousand Sikhs were massacred on the order of Rajiv Gandhi. Within two months, in parliament elections, he won with two-third majority. The present political party in power has used the same strategy. The only difference is that it has replaced Sikhs with Muslims.

The Indian democracy is bloodthirsty. Irrespective of the political affiliation, the Indian democracy needs the heads of a few thousand Sikhs, Muslims, Dalits, Adivasis, leftists, women to keep it alive.

To be or not to be is not the question. The being and the other derive their being from each other. The annihilation of the "other" is the fascist project. It must be opposed by the maximum intellectual incision of the Indian intelligentsia.

The fascists cannot tolerate the young girls wearing jeans and reading Sartre or Marx. Their skulls must be broken. And, they should be held responsible for violence, for after all, if they had not provoked with their "anti-national" acts, the police would not have acted the way it did. The girls who dare cross the thresholds of caste and creed to find their life partners are burnt alive. A large number of the members of our parliament have criminal records. They are their badges of honour. What matters in Indian democracy is money and muscle. It is unfortunate but this is the verity of our political system, and more than that, of the level of awareness of our masses. After all, we must remember that the same democratic forces had executed Socrates, for the same reason. He was teaching the Greek youth, the concepts of justice, truth, human and political rights, reason and logic. He told them that an unexamined life is not worth living.

There is a paradox in the life of JNU. This university is never amicable to the political masters whoever they may be. At the same time, year after year, it is declared to be the best university in the country by the standards of the same government. The other day, the same Minister of Education who had been deriding JNU every day for all the ills of our nation, had to declare that JNU is top university, for in a recent very prestigious all India competition, JNU students had acquired eighteen out of thirty-two positions. In fact, he had forgotten to note that every year, for the most prestigious administrative posts, a considerable number of winners are always from JNU. So, what to do? Destroy the very tree that gives you the fruit of life.

The North Gate of the university is closed. The vans of Delhi police are everywhere. The ruffians of the administrations beat the students and teachers. The police of Delhi is not supposed to see anything other than what the bosses tell it to see and report. The very students, who were beaten, were accused to have been responsible for all the violence. Interestingly, it is not just Delhi police, the police all over the country, in every educational institution, repeats the same discourse. Those who were the objects of violence are held responsible, for creating disturbance. In the beginning of the Republic, Socrates is told that justice is what interests the powerful. It takes Plato, a couple of hundred pages, to reverse this opinion. It will take much more to change the attitude of the powers to be in Bharat and their police to understand, what in fact, is justice, for, as we have seen in recent judgements of our courts, the powerful indeed is always right and just. January is an auspicious month. It is the month of university uprising, of the aspirations of the youth of India. I was born in January. On my birthday, on thirteenth January, 1898, Emile Zola wrote, J'accuse. I retired from JNU in 2000 as Professor Emeritus. I am now eighty-five, good age, to reflect upon things past and present.

What is interesting in this Indian universities uprising is that it is sudden and simultaneous. In a way, it is not so sudden, for the fire was slowly moving to the fore. The wise and sagacious politicians had not bargained for this awareness of the educated youth. They had gained power on the basis of their slogans of 'nation in danger' or 'religion in danger', and it had worked. The soldiers who were killed in their unholy wars were declared martyrs. The corruption reached its zenith when even their coffins were sold...The gullible had voted en mass. Their power was democratic and constitutional. They had manoeuvred well. But enough was enough. The university graduates were not fooled by empty rhetoric. They asked for freedom of thinking and living. Even their own girls were not ready to obey the commands of the elders of the khap panchayats. The young and enlightened children of Bharat were looking far beyond the horizons of the ignorant and the fanatic hordes of RSS.

In India, corruption, lust of power and dynastic ascendency go together. As far as Congress is concerned, it died with Nehru. His daughter appropriated the communal agenda of RSS and declared emergency for the first time in India. Rajiv Gandhi got three thousand Sikhs killed to get parliamentary majority. Now Sonia Gandhi's obsession is to guard the dynastic power for her children, Rahul and Priyanka. There is absolutely no ideology, good or bad, political power is the only goal. All rivals, real or imagined, must be cast away.

There are at least three left parties : CPI,CPIM, and the so-called Maoists. There is intense infighting. Similarly, there are numerous regional and national level parties of the right with all sorts of religiously attractive names. Fortunately, for all of them, the common masses of Bharat have yet not found their hollowness, they are only deluded by their supposed holiness.

The political scenario is bleak, very bleak. This is where the university critique plays its role, however small and insignificant it may appear to be. It is very small but it is certainly not insignificant. The ruthlessness with which the political establishment wants to destroy the university system shows how scared it is of this new awareness. The emergency and immediacy with which the violence is used against innocent students shows that the political masters of Bharat are nervous. They never thought that the educated youth of Bharat, of their Bharat, will rise in unison. They depended on the dichotomy of Muslim versus Hindu. They never realised, that first of all, there are more Muslims in India than in Pakistan. They are more educated and enlightened Muslims in India than in any other Muslim country. The educated Muslim youth has already transcended the religious horizon. It has the same ideas and ideals that every young man or woman of Bharat has. Mandir or Mosque are irrelevant. The youth of India, Muslim or Hindu, is free thinking, free living. It has transcended the narrow lanes of communal bigotry. The Muslim girls are as ambitious and progressive as other girls in India.

Social sciences and structuralism emphasised the importance of the structural, integral constitution of each language or culture. Modern linguistics and anthropology demonstrated how each language, however primitive it was supposed to be, had an internal cohesive structure as perfect and worthy of analysis as any classical language. So was the case with the so-called primitive or tribal cultures. It gave a scientific respectability hitherto ignored for such languages and cultures. In the beginning, it gave rise to the intense debates between those who emphasised synchrony over diachrony or present over past. The incessant debates between Sartre and Lévi-Strauss point in this direction. There was also the question of the tendency of the social scientists to study only the collectivities, societies, groups without paying any attention to the individual within a group. However, it was soon realised that while an individual is a member of a group, she is not dissolved in the group. As a matter of fact, as in my own case, the understanding of cohesive linguistic structures led me to a much better understanding of historical, classical texts and their authors. It is this quest that led me first to go back to the Cartesian period, Port Royal Logic and Grammar, and to the Abélardian theory of language of the twelfth century. I continued my quest and discovered several corresponding theoretical insights of the Nayaya Vaishishika school with modern propositions of structure and system. It was further reinforced with the comparative, typological study of the Buddhist philosophers of language with the *sphota* of Bhartrihari. Also, very interestingly, within the same tradition, how radically Bhartrihari differed with the other great grammarian, Panini. It is so enriching to compare the materialism of Samkhya with that of Aristotle, and so on...No thinker of any tradition is a foreigner to a student of thought. Greek, European, Hindu, Muslim, Christian,

Buddhist and so many other traditions have had great thinkers, who were all very critical of their ancestors. None can be so opposed to each other as Plato and Aristotle in Greek thought. The same is true in other traditions of philosophical reflection. Unfortunately, the so-called "nationalists" try to present these traditions as homogenous parameters. There is no such thing in the history of ideas. To be human is to think, and to think, differently, critically. To belong to any religion or a political party is to renounce being human. Thinking beings transcend these hermetically sealed sects.

This is the role that JNU has played, that every university in this country, is playing. This is the role of enlightenment, of logic, of reason. The same role that once the enlightened ancient Indian sages and philosophers played, the same role that the Muslim thinkers of the ninth century played, to not only enlighten the Muslim world, but the whole world with their most incisive interpretations of Plato and Aristotle that finally led to the emergence of Renaissance in Europe. It is the same role that Descartes and Rousseau played that led to the eighteenth century French revolution, to the twentieth century May 68 movement in France. JNU and the Indian universities have inherited all this and more. They are now the harbingers of new enlightenment, of new awareness of what is just and right, what is pure and impure, what is profane and sacred. The most sacred is the human right, the right to equality of gender and race, the right to free thinking and free living.

Sir, what do you think of the Noble prizes given every year, once a student asked me. Well, the intention of the Noble Foundation cannot be doubted. They are sincere and honest. The only problem is the frequency with which these awards are given. Now you cannot have a great theoretician every year. In mathematics, the equivalent award is given every four years. It has acquired a certain prestige. I believe that if the Noble is awarded every five years, it will carry with it the honour and prestige, it is supposed to have. Take for example, the case of literature. There were noble laureates like Tagore, Hemingway, Camus and Sartre. There have been so many before and since then. Who knows them? I do not think even the students of literature can remember the names of the last five of these. Noble prizes are following the model of fast food. We must realise that intellectual pursuit is a slow and steady process. Theoretical breakthroughs happen only once in a while. You can even call it aristocratic. Yes, it is aristocracy but the aristocracy of the intellect. The professors of JNU are materially comfortable but not rich, like the university professors all over the world. In my parties, on the menu, there was always one item, the pakoras. We celebrated doctoral theses, seminar debates, it was not the celebration of body and leisure. It is interesting to note that practically none of the great thinkers of the modern world was awarded a noble prize. They all lived a materially comfortable but not very rich life. In that aristocratic ambience, they revolutionised the world of ideas. The JNU intelligentsia continues that tradition.

Another problem with the Noble awards is that they are stuck in the Western tradition. It is probably fine as far as the physical sciences are concerned. In literature, for example, there are very outstanding writers in regional languages in India who are far better than most of those who get Noble every year. Because of their non-western linguistic and cultural tradition, they are not so well known.

As far as the political and communal establishment is concerned, it cannot be allowed by the present establishment. It is contagious. All these young men and women will go astray. They will all become "anti-national". This has to be stopped. They have tried other persuasive means. They have not worked. Now violence is the only way out. Come what may, the rule of law, their law, must be imposed, whether these young fellows are willing or not, does not matter.

When Aishe Ghosh, the president of the students union of JNU was hit on the head and was bleeding, Delhi police was busy filing FIR against her for her participation in the violence in the university. This girl is brave and enlightened. So are the girls of other universities. Interestingly, in this uprising, there are more girls than boys all over. In demonstration after demonstration for civil liberties, the girls and women of India are taking a decisive lead. This is the most frightening aspect of this movement. As far as I can see, the future belongs to the girls of India. I know this is a nightmare for the RSS ideologues.

In all universities, in every class, in every discipline, there are more girls than boys. Already, in all branches of civil service, there are many women. This is going to grow. A day is not very far when the civil service of Bharat will be run by these girls. The old order will cede to the new. These highly educated and enlightened souls will not accept the dictates of the old order, the order of the khap panchayats, the order of mothers-in-law, the order of those who believe that there was plastic surgery in ancient India, the Kaurvas were test-tube babies, the arrows of Arjun had nuclear tips, the udan khatolas of yonder days were in fact air planes, etc., etc. The Indian Civil Service will be inundated by these girls and the ministers will come begging to get their dirty deeds washed by fake papers.

It is a wonderful experience to meet these young IAS officers. Once when I was in Shimla at the Institute of Advanced Study, a girl phoned me from the office, if she could see me. Yes, of course. When she arrived, I recognised her as one of my old students. I thought she was a tourist visiting Shimla. No, she was already an IAS officer and was posted in Himachal Pradesh. I looked at her and could not help saying, you are now an IAS officer, why don't you dress like one. No, sir, I was a JNU girl, I will always remain a JNU girl, simple and honest. When these girls take over Indian Civil Service, our society will be more civilised, more gentle, more well behaved.

At Shimla, I also taught the children of the Secretary of the Institute the art of French cooking. They learnt how to make a grog, a concoction of hot water, rum and honey; Irish coffee with dark, strong black coffee and whisky; and the roasting of pheasant, rabbit, fish, chicken and mutton.

Once I read in a newspaper a notice about a housing society in Patna where not only the IAS officers, but only the JNUite IAS officers, were allowed. Obviously, there must have been enough JUNites to have so many flats to themselves. Imagine when their gender will also change, a change that is on the horizon of Bharat.

The January uprising has many facets. Locally, there were problems of fee hike, decrease in the number of research students. The M Phil and Ph D seats were kept unfulfilled. M A is o k. The students leave after two years but once they become research scholars, they stay for ever, for six years. It is too long. It is in this period that the students come under the influence of different ideologies. Education and enlightenment cross the thresholds set by our elders, the gurus of yonder days.

One of the reasons of JNU uprising was the hike in price of the hostel charges. The food in all hostels everywhere is horrible but the case of JNU is unique. Compared with fairly homogenous students' communities, JNU students come from all over Bharat. Every kitchen in the JNU hostel has to cater to at least five food habits. As a result, what the students get is a sort of admixture, a "national" food that has not only no taste but it is inedible. On top of it, the administration asks the students to pay several times more than what they are used to. No wonder, they are furious.

The administration and the government tried to calm down the situation by accepting one demand or the other. Naturally, this did not satisfy the students. The agitation continued. The authorities blamed the students who kept on changing their goals. What was never realised that these small local problems was not the issue. What was at stake was the very spirit of the university. The basic question was, and is, what is a university, what it stands for, what are its ideals, the ideals for which the students of all universities since ages past have been struggling.

This reminds me of my favourite French philosopher, Pierre Abélard, of the twelfth century, who rebelled against the ecclesiastic authorities. He was ex-communicated twice. His writings were burnt in Rome and he was sent to a monastery to spend his life in seclusion. Abélard was the student leader of the twelfth century. He left the right bank of Notre Dame and walked over to Montagne Sainte Genviève, on the left bank. Since then, this Left Bank or Latin Quarter became the lieu of all contestations and controversies. The nomenclature, Left, is also due to this move. This is why I have included my paper written several years ago on this theme. It sets the genealogy of our student movements.

It all started in 1963. With a doctorate in linguistics from the United States under Professor Henry Allan Gleason Jr. I was awarded a research fellowship, Attaché de Recherche, at the Centre National de la Recherche Scientifique, Paris, with the recommendation of Professor André Martinet of the Sorbonne. Officially, I was supposed to do field work in the French Alps in a village, called, Beaufort-sur-Doron near Albertville. I used to go there very often. Soon I acquired a working knowledge of the local patois. My informant was an old soldier who had fought in the first world war. His narratives of hunting always ended in failure. Nothing was ever caught. His last sentence was : this is life ! I was in my twenties. I received this wisdom form an old man in his seventies. Only the scoundrels succeed. The hunters, the students, the scholars only chase a horizon that remains always at a respectable distance.

I stayed mostly in Paris, and in the French system of higher education, one does not need any enrolment, I followed the lectures of Lévi-Strauss, Beneveniste and Greimas at the Collège de France, of Martinet at the Sorbonne, of Althusser at the Ecole Normale, and of course, of Sartre in the public domain. Later on when Foucault and Roland Barthes joined Collège de France, I listened to them for years. Lacan was an invitee of

Althusser at the Ecole, so the students went there for his very complex discourses. It was a very different experience from the United States where every thing was so rigid and strict. The Latin Quarter is indeed a great place for free learning and discussion. I tried to create the same intellectual atmosphere at JNU.

From the structuralist movement of the sixties, I moved on to the Cartesian period of the seventeenth and eighteenth century. There was the Cartesian method, the Cartesian theory of innate ideas, which Chomsky misinterpreted in his Cartesian linguistics. What Chomsky never understood was the following debate in Port Royal, Condillac and Destut de Tracy. Another ridiculous situation was that of Derrida in his Grammatology. He borrowed heavily from Condillac without duly acknowledging it. The so-called "deconstruction" is a concept directly derived from Condillac. Derrida had a very poor background in linguistics. He messed up the differences in oral and written registers of language without realising that there is no binary opposition between the two. There is in fact a dialectical relation. Both engage and enrich each other. Foucault and Derrida were both students of Althusser, this did not deter them to go in radically different directions.

It is in this period of my research, especially in the linguistic theories of Port Royal that my attention was drawn to the writings of the twelfth century French philosopher, Pierre Abélard. As I went through the classical interpretation of Abélardian theory of language by Jean Jolivet, I spent several years of study in this domain. In the famous controversy around "universals", Abélard proposed a middle path between Platonic realism of imaginary forms and the Aristotelian nominalism of the physical reality of individual, specific objects. We begin with a sensuous experience, followed by *imaginatio* and *intellectus*. For Abélard, the Aristotelian proposition is a good point of departure but it must be followed by the reconstruction of this experience in the domain of imaginaire for an analytical articulation. This theory of Abélard, combined with the propositions of Port Royal and Condillac, Merleau-Ponty, Althusser and Foucault, became my theoretical basis for all discursive analysis. I attempted to apply it in domains very different from what it was supposed to be.

It gave me a theory of Discourse that could cover any text, oral or written, artistic or discursive, in any form, in any style. With this methodology, I presented a long monograph on the semiotics of discourse of Gustave Flaubert's Saint Julien. This study became a model for several doctoral theses of my students. My method was deductive. It could be applied to any text, written or visual. Whatever be the discursive form, the central theme is invariably existential. In every case, it is the human existence, that is at stake. The "condition humaine" is what we must discern and describe. This is where Sartre is most relevant.

A student of German Centre wanted to work on Kafka. Together we read all the texts of Kafka. We analysed Metamorphosis and Trial. We saw some human conflicts and contradictions that the earlier critics had not referred to. She is now an associate professor in the same Centre.

A number of students worked on the cinematographic texts of Bengali films, especially of Ritwik Ghatak. I was not at all familiar with these texts. Together we discussed these narratives, their motifs, their symbolism, their human, existential predicaments. The students wrote excellent theses. The first one has gone on a tangent, with the same theoretical finesse, he has acquired a very sophisticated understanding of Sufism, its music and philosophy. The other two are professors of English in Jamia and Ambedkar. There is another very interesting case of a student who showed interest in the philosophy and psychology in the plays of Shakespeare. I suggested, he should read Lacan. At present, he is one of the most important scholars of Lacan. Recently, he organised an international seminar on Lacan and asked me to inaugurate it. I was scared. My interest in Lacan had diminished. I was more occupied with Sartre, Merleau-Ponty, Foucault, Lévi-Strauss and Althusser. I somehow convinced him that I could not come. When he edited the proceedings of the seminar, he dedicated them to me saying that once I had suggested that he should read Lacan, he has done nothing but reading Lacan since then. How charming and nice of him for giving me the credit for doing practically nothing. His thesis was entitled, The predicament of instability – the mechanism of metaphor and metonymy in Christopher Marlow's the tragical historic of Doctor Faustus. He is now a professor of English at Jadavpur.

Then there was the case of a student, very well versed in philosophy, whose thesis was on the Pragmatics of Death in the figures of Socrates Antigone and Jesus. He is now a professor in the Centre of Arts and Aesthetics. Another student analysed the Tempest of Shakespeare with Abélardian critique and neo-Platonic metaphysics. He is now professor of English in Central University of Kerala. Also. Mousumi Biswas : The semiotics of feminine discourse in Gustave Flaubert's Madame Bovary. Bela Cheema : The semiotics of human condition and violence in Indian cinema

There is also the case of the student who never finished his thesis, for after writing four hundred pages, he called it only an introduction. He was the brightest of them all.

Those who never complete their theses are generally the most brilliant. They search for a theoretical breakthrough that always eludes them.

There are numerous such examples. At JNU the research is mutual and participatory. The students and teachers are equally involved. I have learnt a lot from my students. Whether they have or not, I do not know.

What is important to emphasise here is the importance that philosophy plays in French scholarship. Instead of the Anglo-saxon interest in the formal structures of language, its phonology, morphology and syntax, it is the philosophy of language that is the central concern. Similarly, every literary, cultural, artistic text is basically a philosophical text, and it is discerned and analysed as such. My general impression is that the students of JNU take their educational pursuits seriously. They are not there just to pass exams but their aim is enlightenment in every sense of the term.

There were students who were involved in more theoretical work. One of them did an extremely incisive thesis on Foucault. Another is now an authority on German philosophy. His books are being published by the Edinburgh University Press. Both of them are now professors in their own Centre. Another student worked on the feminist condition. She now heads a relevant department at Jamia. All of them surpassed my work in incision and rigour.

At Patiala, before I joined JNU, the heavily charged leftist movement did not deter students from being engaged in meticulous studies of literature and culture. There were theses on Hemingway, Raja Rao, R. K. Narayan along with the studies of Punjabi legends and myths, of Sanjhi, Mirza Sahiban, Puran Bhagat, even of the ceremonies of birth and death. Most of these scholar students retired as professors from our prestigious universities. At eighty-five, I am so old now. There is only the nostalgia and the memory, almost in Lacanian terms.

The stay at JNU is a very significant period in the life of the students. They do not want to waste it in superficial accumulation of general knowledge. Knowledge, for them, is primarily a means to enlightenment, to live and breathe in the universe of ideas. It is this pursuit that frightens the establishment, the politically naïve masters of fanaticism.

This is an autobiographical note. It is not unique in any sense of the term. Almost all professors of JNU have had similar intellectual journeys.

The North Gate of Jawaharlal Nehru University is shut. There are barricades all over. The police vans are moving in and out side of the vast and wild campus without finding their way in any direction. There are nil gais, peacocks, jackals, foxes and serpents. There are also students and professors discussing and debating surrealistic, intellectual and political ideas in class rooms, hostels and dhabas. The North Gate is shut... There is No Exit.

भाषा, साहित्य एवं संस्कृति अध्ययन संस्थान-I
SCHOOL OF LANGUAGE, LITERATURE & CULTURE STUDIES-I
ABVP WELCOME FRESHERS
KASHMIR
AISF
ABVP
ABVP
EXPLODE
AiSf

खाना उनका
सड़क हमारी
कारें उनकी
संसद में सरकारें उनकी
AISA
Where you can enslave fellow humans and Plunder the planet— and be praised for your good business sense.
SMASH CAPITALISM
aisa
ABVP
PEOPLE'S MARCH TO SAVE DEMOCRACY
PEOPLE'S MARCH TO SAVE DEMOCRACY

कहाँ ला सुतल बाटे सुनत न
डोम जानी हमनी के छुए से
हमनी के इनरा के निगीचे ना
पांकी में से भरी भरी पियतानी
पनही से पीटी पीटी हाथ गोड़
हमनी के इतना काहे को
हमनी रात दिन दुखवा
हमनी के साहेबे से मिनती
FIGHT
Caste
Violence
Women

Saluting Saadat Hasan Manto on his Birth
"Dear Uncle Sam...
...You should know why my country sliced away from India, came in to being and
which is why I am taking the liberty of writing to you...
...Uncle, I will not labour the point since an all knowing seer like you can well
...dom of a bird whose wings have been clipped can enjoy
...as far your military pact with us, it is remarkable and should be
You should sign something similar with India. Sell all your old
the two of us, the ones you used in the last war.
This junk will thus be off your hands and your armament factories
longer remain idle..."
- from Manto's Letters to Uncle Sam
aisa

# STAY HOME, GO HOME

Those who have a home, stay home, those who do not, dream of going home. The daily wagers, bereft of their wages, destitute and alienated, want to go home. They walk hundreds of miles, barefoot, accompanied by their little ones, wives and mothers, through thick and thin to a home that is not only far away, it may never be reached. Several of them died before they could meet their loved ones. Their existential anguish is beyond the bourgeois imagination. A home is a home, however poor and wretched it may be. It is place of solace, spiritual peace, to be with one's own, children, parents, friends. The State refuses to accept them, orders them to stay where they are, for, the State has no provisions to feed them, give any medicine. The State believes that the whole State, physical as well as cultural, belongs to them. No body has a right to his home. All homes belong to the State. None can move to and fro his domicile.

The State and those who have comfortable homes cannot imagine that even the have-nots can dream of a home. When the poor are hungry, destitute and alienated, their need of a home is not just physical, it is existential. It is much more charged with anguish than the anguish and anxiety of Sartrean existentialism that is primarily concerned with the European bourgeoisie's anxieties. When we see the images of a young man sharing his bowl of rice with his two children, wife and mother, to walk along the rest of the day without rest or respite, there is no upheaval within us, no feeling of a sad and suffering humanity. The State and the employers are only worried about when he will come back to serve them again. Again and again, they keep on counting their workload without paying him anything during his lay-off.

The daily wager is simply not a human being. He is a number and a figure. The State bothers only about the work he can and must do.

He is paid the minimum possible, just to physically stay alive, just to be there at the service of the employer. When the required work is completed, he is thrown away, discarded like a squeezed orange. That he is also a human being, has human feelings of affection and endearment, of family and friends, is beyond the imagination of the one who can hire him whenever he needs. The State and the employers keep on changing their minds, stay home, go home. Every other day, the order changes.

There are trains, there are no trains. One State allows them, the other tells them, they are not welcome. Even the trains keep on changing their schedule. There is no policy, just the whim of the master.

# THINKING AND COGNITION

Thinking is reflecting, discerning, an effort to know the other, in a way, to think about the other, the other who is not known or not knowable. The being and the other are in a dialectical relationship. They want to know each other. The other is beautiful, intelligent, always smiling, gentle and affectionate. I love her. She loves me. She is very sincere. So am I. And, so on... But what does it all mean? I am not sure. I am a thinking being. I always think. Thinking is a nuisance. It makes me restless, hesitant, confused. I want to live with the other. But when I live with the other, I want to live alone, in peace and harmony, with my self. The being can neither live with nor without the other. It is a paradox. There is no solution. The being keeps on thinking, thinking endlessly, eternally.

Language and thinking go together. The twelfth century philosopher, Abélard, tells me that the the word leads to the idea, the idea to the thing. My word, my enunciation leads me to the idea of the object I am thinking of, which enables me to discern the object. To discern is to be in the universe of ideas, in the universe of thinking. It is an abstract world. But it also corresponds to a manifest world. The world within and the world without are in a certain dialectical relation. The being and the other are not independent. They are continuously, eternally dialectically engaged with each other. Sartre did not say, to be OR not to be. He emphasised the Being AND Néant, the being AND not being. There is an opposition but there is also a relation. In this unending relation and non-relation, one is never sure of oneself. There is the eternal Doubt that is pregnant with the germs of all discerning. Dubito, ergo, Deus est. I doubt, therefore, God is. The seventeenth century Port Royal Logic complicates the signifying act much further when it underscores that when we enunciate a word, it has a certain resonance which is already a signifier, which, in turn, leads not to the object being discerned, but to the image of the object. We move from the resonance of the word to the image of the object. The signifying correlation then is between resonance and image and not between the word and the object. In other words, the signifying process becomes more and more abstract.

We are in the domain of what Merleau-Ponty calls the *pensée pensante*, the thinking thought, thought in the process of being thought. As a result, the discourse of the creative writer is a specific articulation of a specific perception of a specific existentialist experience. At each step, there is thinking, there is specific existential realisation of what is discerned and what is expressed. There is also, as Merleau-Ponty says, the dialectic of the *parole parlante* and the *pensée pensante*, of the speaking speech and the thinking thought. The speaking subject and the thinking subject interact with each other both dialectically and in association. The words of the creative writer are charged with her perception, with her extremely personal existential experience inflected with the perpetual pulls and pushes of the simultaneous thinking act. The Word is the World, says Merleau-Ponty. In Sausurrean terms, in the signifying act, the *signifiant* and the *signifié*, are not independent references, signification lies in the fusion of the signifier and the signified. This is an ideal situation. The being and the other lose their very beings in this highly charged universe of signifying creativity. In other words, there is no more a dialectic of the being and the other. The world within and the world without become one unified entity. It is the highest form of this paradox.

Whether we follow the tertiary definition of Abélard or the quaternary definition of Port Royal, one thing is certain that whatever significance the word had at the point of departure is lost or modified in the signifying act. In the praxis of the *parole parlante* and the *pensée pensante*, the speaking speech and the thinking thought, we may use the same words but we do not use them with the same significance as the others do. As a result, says Condillac, we are hermetically sealed in our own universe. Linguistically, we are now prisoners of our own selves. The being and the other are blocked in this absolute disharmony.

But all is not lost. There is no such thing as an isolated world within. The world within must reflect upon the world without even for its own existence. There is no escape from their dialectical interaction. No doubt, there are hindrances, there are obstacles, there are associations, there are transgressions but ultimately the being has to live with the other however painful it may be. In Sartrean terms, there is no exit.

As long as human beings are endowed with the faculty of thinking, they are human as opposed to those who do not think. *Je pense donc je suis*. I think, therefore, I am. Even in the French tradition, this is how Descartes' COGITO ERGO SUM is rendered. But this is not what Descartes said. Cogito is "I cognise". Thinking is after all an intellectual activity. To cognise transcends this threshold. In an absolute existential analysis, cognition is far more significant than thinking. "Thinking" is easily understood at the popular level. In the subtitle of the book on Method, Descartes wrote that he had rendered it into the language of the people, that is French, so that even peasants and women may also learn how to reason. I am sorry, our discussion in this seminar is held at a slightly different level. Let us then interpret this thinking thought in the suspended binary of cognition and thinking. We must use the term, thinking, but we should be aware that the French philosopher had perhaps intended some other conceptualisation, not very different, but also certainly not identical.

Let us go back to the creative act. The creative discourse as I referred to earlier is a specific articulation of a specific perception of a specific existential experience. The point of departure is a specific existential experience. It means that even at this juncture, we are dealing with a personal, individual, existential perception. of an event or a contact or a confrontation with the other. It goes through the sieve of perception, discerning in the domain of the imaginaire where in the *kalpana* of the Buddhists, there is a certain reorganisation, a certain reconstitution of the universe of facts.

Words and Concepts, šabad and vikalp are dialectically engaged with each other :

vikalpa-yonayaḥ šabdāḥ
vikalpāḥ šabda-yonayaḥ

In this domain, the role of memory is very important, for in this tradition, all reality is in flux. Our first contact lapses into past as soon as it is realised in the present. Now the memory of something is similar but never identical with the first encounter. Once the creative writer has constituted a specific universe, she renders it into a specific articulation. This articulation or rather this enunciation follows the grammatical rules of the language but as the discourse is a conceptual construct, it formulates its own thresholds. As Spinoza said, we move from the universe of facts to the universe of concepts. According to Althusser, even Marx had made a clear distinction between economy and the concept of economy which most of the modern Marxists have either ignored or forgotten.

What is articulated then is how an event, an encounter, is perceived, discerned. This cannot be taken as an historical document. It follows the method of archaeology where several pieces are put together in the jigsaw puzzle for future discourses. The linearity of the historical progression is subjected to the archaeological non-linearity. We move from the syntagmatic presentations to the paradigmatic, metaphoric articulations. The enunciative discourses are always constituted in this ideological movement of going back and forth whether it is a matter of the in-conscience (sub conscience) as Lacan would have it or as the Archaeology of Knowledge as presented by Foucault.

The creative act is not factual, it is conceptual. It is not metonymic, it is metaphoric. It is very fashionable these days for social scientists and journalists to analyse creative texts to arrive at historical discourses. It defies the very nature of the creative act. For example, there have been recently several attempts by the historians to interpret Saadat Hassan Manto's stories on the partition of India. This becomes evident when such texts are translated. The last sentence of Manto's narrative, Tobha Tek Singh, *wahan parha tha Tobha Tek Singh*, is translated by Khushwant Singh as "there lay the body of Bishan Singh of the village of Tobha Tek Singh". Now, Manto's sentence stated simply, "there lay Tobha Tek Singh". The translator is trying to explain to the readers, who is lying there, who may not have understood such a simple sentence. He never realised that Tobha Tek Singh was no more the name of a place or a person. Manto had constituted, in this short narrative, *Tobha Tek Singh*, as a metaphor of the absolute absurdity of the partition of the country. *Tobha Tek Singh* was now lying in no man's land on both sides of which were the absurd entities of India and Pakistan. Since Partition, all Indian and Pakistani Punjabis are mentally lying in this no-man's land, and so are the Bengalis on both sides of the border, in spite of all the efforts of the fanatic despots to divide them. Our fundamentalist ideologues were surprised when the Eastern Bengalis fought for the Bengali language as their most cherished heritage. Unfortunately, it has not been so, at least not to that extent, in West Punjab.

The universe of *Tobha Tek Singh* is a mental asylum. There is the world within the asylum, where the *mad* persons talk sense, and the world without the asylum, which is infested with murder and plunder, the world where the populace under the heavy dose of fanaticism has lost all senses... There is another very significant narrative of Manto, *Thanda Gosht*, The Cold Flesh, where in the same universe of massacres and molestations, a ruthless brute, a beast, stunned by the corpse of a young girl in his arms, loses all physical and sexual appetite, and *becomes human.* Both these texts are highly existential discourses on the complexity of human paradoxes. In literary creativity, these narratives transcend Urdu and Indian literature and can be compared with the best of world literature.

If the relation of the being with the other is existential, it can only be cognitive. It cannot be a resultant of a "thinking" activity. Thinking is by and large intellectual, even logical. The existential dimension goes far beyond the intellectual. In a way, it transcends thinking. The bond between the being and the other is existential. They cannot exist one without the other. If there is no being, there is no other. Even if we remove the tags of being and other, subject and object, and just have *a* and *b*, it is obvious that *a* and *b* derive their beings from each other. The subject and the object, the being and the other, keep on reversing their roles. And even if this relation is dialectical, it is more cognitive than logical.

If Descartes used the Latin term, COGITO, it was not for nothing. If for the sake of argument, we may pose suspension or hesitation between these two concepts, our reflection cannot be conclusive, and for good reason.

Let us go back to literary creativity. For me the point of departure for any creative activity is existential. There is a dialectical relation between the world within and the world without. One cannot exist without the other. For social scientists, only the world without exists. All facts, all beings, are anonymous, they can easily be covered with historical, socio-economic conditions. In this perspective, there is no such thing as a being. It is only the figment of imagination of the bourgeois. It is in this context that Sartre asks a question : Paul Valery is a petit-bourgeois intellectual, that is certain, but every petit-bourgeois intellectual is not Paul Valery. The Marxist critique, and all other social sciences for that matter, do not have the mediatory thresholds to discern and describe this paradox. But this is the most important paradox.

In terms of Merleau-Ponty, we begin with the speaking subject who learns language and culture of her environment as a given but as the speaking subject slowly grows into a thinking subject she begins to appropriate language and culture in a specific, existential manner. Finally, she uses the language charged with signifiers which are very personal and perceptive. This a resultant of a series of existential and intellectual experiences which the writer shares with none. There is as such the intellectual and ideological specific path of the author as the ideological path of Marx as discerned by Althusser. From his early dissertations to Das Capital we follow the path of Marx when slowly and steadily Marx becomes Marxist.

I would like to end this note with the relationship of the being and the other as two beings in love. Now, what does “love” mean between two beings? I am inspired by the quaternary definition of signification of the seventeenth century Port Royal monks. For each word, there is the resonance of the word, which is highly significant in itself,which refers not to the object, but to the image of the object. In the case of the two beings, there are two worlds which interact with each other in the domain of the imaginaire. With the worlds without, there are forms and images. With the worlds within, there are perceptions and reflections. Now this within and without must interact with each other both dialectically and associationally.

If there is harmony and accord, the worlds within and the worlds without follow the same rhyme and reason, if not, the harmonious edifice falls apart.
But fall is the necessary condition for resurrection!
We are suspended between Cogito and Dubito? Cartesian cognition/thinking leads to the existence of the being. Cartesian doubt leads to the existence of God and Love.

COGITO  ERGO SUM
DUBITO ERGO DEUS EST
DUBITO ERGO AMOR EST

# THE MYTH OF THE GREAT PROFESSOR AND THE GOOD STUDENT

(The Semiotics of the students' movement of May 1968 in France)

The events of May 1968 in France have been commented upon by numerous analysts, and all these commentaries can be justifiably considered logical in the French sense of the term. Before I attempt to present my interpretation of the affair, here is a brief account of the narrative.

In 1968, there were five main active groups of students in France. The UNEF or L'Union Nationale des Etudiants de France, which had been in existence ever since the end of the Second World War, was a highly politicised and divided body of students which took part in the events of Algeria, Vietnam, and had reacted to numerous upheavals in eastern Europe. The rivalries in this Union had given rise to other groups. One such group was CLEAR or the Comité de Liaison des Etudiants Révolutionnaires, which was inspired by Trotskyism and the themes of the Fourth International. Another group called itself JCR or the Jeunesse Communiste Révolutionnaire. It also followed Trotsky but it was a separate group. The fourth group was CVN or the Comité Vietnam Nationale, organized by Laurent Schwartz and Alain Krivine. Jean- Paul Sartre had also been associated with it. And lastly, there were the UJCML or the L'Union de Jeunesse Communistes Marxistes Leninistes, composed of the pro-Chinese Marxist students. We can add to this list the movement of March 22, founded by Daniel Cohn-Bendit at Nanterre.

Our narrative begins on twenty-second of March when the students of Nanterre occupy the Tower of the Faculty, and declare war on French educational and cultural system. On March 28, Nanterre is closed, and, on the following day, the Nanterre campus, few miles away from Paris, is occupied by the students. As the studies are discontinued, the students swarm the Latin Quarter, the lieu of the Sorbonne and the great battles of students against the authority since the twelfth century. One is immediately reminded of the romantic and tumultuous union of Abélard and Héloïse, and all the strikes of the monk students and the fierce battles on horsebacks against the established authorities of the Church and the King.
The traditional May first demonstrations took place from the Republique Square to that of the Bastille by a combined force of the workers unions, the Communist Party and the socialists, COT, PC, and PSU. On May second, all work at Nanterre campus is stopped, and, on the third, the police occupies the Sorbonne, and all teaching is suspended. The sixth of May witnesses the first barricades in the Latin Quarter, and, the students" movement spreads to the campuses of the provincial universities, especially Strasbourg and Nantes. Between May 7 and 9, the University rectorate tries to negotiate peace with the students but fails. On May 10, the whole of the Latin Quarter is occupied by hundreds of thousands of students. There are barricades all over, and, all night there are skirmishes between the police and the students. The molotoves and street stones are freely hurled at the bourgeoisie and its guardian police. The following day, on May 11, several workers unions decide for a general strike on May 13. The Censier Centre of the University is occupied by the students. The Prime Minister, George Pompidou, who was away in Afghanistan, returns to Paris. There are some measures of reconciliation and a few arrested students are released, but this has no effect on the movement. On May 13, the Sorbonne is occupied by the students and the workers go on a general strike of twenty-four hours.
Strangely enough, as nothing serious was happening in Paris, de Gaulle leaves on an official visit to Romania on May 14. The same day, the workers are on strike all over France. On May 15, the students occupy the theatre Odeon. By May 17, ten million workers are on strike. In other words, one out of every five Frenchmen has stopped working. This is the biggest strike ever in the history of

France. On May 26, suddenly there is no petrol in Paris. So nobody can move. There is perfect immobility. The Sartrean hell is enacted for all to confront each other. Since there is no exit, there is violence. The revolution is let loose by the students and the young workers. All established parties, on the right or left, are taken by surprise, and are reluctant to take part in this tumult. The movement, however" is so overwhelming that they hesitatingly begin to join in the revolutionary fête. The Communist Party, PC, openly denounces the revolutionary adventurism and pleads for the path of "legality". Pierre Mendes France and François Mitterand are also caught in the same predicament. On May 30, de Gaulle dissolves the National Assembly, and announces new elections. The established left forces are divided. The Gaullists win an overwhelming majority in the Assembly. The communists lose heavily. The good guys are rewarded and the bad boys are punished. For some, the old order was re-established. For others, the revolution was betrayed.

II

The events of May '68 have had microscopic analyses. Amongst the causes of this eruption of student revolt, there have been usual explanations, like the extremely rapid growth of student community, modern industrialisation, the alienating consumers society, and, of course the atmosphere of students contestation all over the world, Berkely, Tokyo, Peking are frequently cited as instances of this phenomenon. While we cannot deny the validity of these arguments, and, it is also obvious that all these oppressive and contagious factors had their influence on the French youth, one cannot stay within a given time and space of synchronic character, the conceptual structures not only interact with each other on the syntagmatic plane, they are not independent entities suspended in air, the dynamic character of the emerging structures must also be found in the historical depths of metaphoric relations. There is no doubt that the French students were inspired by the events in Berkely and Peking, but once the students occupied the holy precincts of the Sorbonne, the French University tradition weighed heavily on them. The walls of Latin Quarter had echoed the revolutionary slogans since the twelfth century. Moreover, the problems that the French students were faced with were very different from those of any other university or country, and naturally, the generating process also followed a different course. In no other country the students movement brought a total chaos in its body politic. Within two weeks of the barricades of the Latin Quarter, ten million young workers had forced the establishment or their unions to come out in the streets and the whole administrative machine was completely paralysed. The concept of total revolution is a typically French phenomenon.

## III

The French University system is a unique adventure. There are only chairs, and the professors are co-opted by the assembly of the professors. There is no advertisement, no selection committee, no body can apply. A scholar who has made a mark in a certain field is invited to grace a chair. At times, a chair may carry the traditional title, as for example, Histoire des idées, at others, a chair is denominated according to the discipline of the invitee, as for example, was the case with Roland Barthes whose chair was christened, the Chair of Semiology. There are no departments, there are only professors and assistants. Once a professor is appointed, there is absolutely no control over his teaching or his evaluation of the students. Until very recent times, there was only one professor in a discipline in the whole country, and his Chair was generally in Paris. A professor often pronounces his discourse before several hundred auditors in an amphitheatre. There is no fee, no enrolment to attend lectures. A professor delivers a Cours Magistral. There are no boards of studies, no syllabus prescribing bodies. A professor is free to programme his lectures any way he likes. At the end of the year, after delivering a .maximum of four lectures a week for about five months, he gives his examination, which always consists of one question, called dissertation, to be answered in four hours. Traditionally, the evaluation results in ninety per cent failure, sometimes even more. The doctoral theses for the State Doctorate take about ten to fifteen years of preparation and include two theses, the principal and the complementary. The defence or viva voce examination is conducted by a jury of at least five professors and usually lasts from five to seven hours. A doctoral thesis in Humanities and Letters is such a rare phenomenon that the reports of the defence are carried in all major newspapers. While there are examinations at the Sorbonne for Licence, the freedom of teaching and learning is unlimited at the Ecole des Hautes Etudes and the Collège de France, where the venerable professors are supposed only to enlighten the auditors with their learning and intellectual brilliance. As the lectures are delivered in large auditoriums, and since there is no enrolment, the competition is merciless. For example, to listen to Michel Foucault or Roland Barthes, one had to go there at least an hour in advance to be able to get a place to sit on the floor. Very often in Foucault's lectures, besides the several hundred occupied seats, there was never any vacant place even to sit on the floor or to stand near the main gate. But the reverse is equally true. There are professors who address empty chairs. Even the great of yonder days have to struggle hard to keep up with their own reputation. While the situation described above for Foucault and Roland Barthes during the years 1979-80 was, by and large, true of Lévi-Strauss and André Martinet in the sixties, the audience for them during these years of my stay in France was just about respectable. It is a free world. One has to keep up with the changing times with considerable intellectual effort. As far as the government is concerned, the professors can teach for ever, they need not retire, so the actual retirement is mental and not physical. In other words, a professor can teach whatever he likes, for as long as he cares to do so, provided of course, he can find an audience. As there is no prescribed course of study, the professors at the Ecole des Hautes Etudes and the Collège de France have to prepare a new course of lectures every year to keep the same pitch of intellectual discourse. This extreme mental strain can be endured only for a few years, and as the professor becomes repetitive or demoded, the disciples begin to desert the guru.

All this began in the year of Lord 1100 when Abélard defeated Guillaume de Champeaux in an open debate at the Ile de la Cité and walked over to the left bank of the river Seine with the students shouting, Maître Pierre avec nous, and founded the School of

Dialectics in this quarter, later called, the Latin Quarter, for Latin was the medium of discourse. Somewhat on the lines of conceptual structuralism and empiricism, the intellectual debate during these days was around the Nominalists and the Realists. For the former, the notions of love, humanity and virtue have no tangible existence, they are simple vocables. For the realists the abstractions, the universals represent essence and thus have a positive life. Abélard defeated the champion of the nominalists, the chanoine of Compiegne, Jean Roscelin, and the chanoine Guillaume de Champeaux, the substantialist. According to Abélard, the universal is not a simple word, nor it is a reality in itself which can have its proper life. What is it then? It is a conception of the esprit, replies Abélard. As Abélard does not have the Licence to teach, he leaves Paris and installs his little university at Corbeil, at a distance of a few miles from the Capital. Guillaume de Champeaux is left alone, his discourses are listened to only by a few faithful students. The large majority of the students, many of them foreigners from the different lands of Christendom, gather around Abélard, and soon the number grows to three thousand. After a few years, Abélard gets the Licence to teach from the successor of Champeaux, and begins to pronounce his discourses on the Montagne Sainte-Geneviève. The students from Brittany, England, Germany, Picardy and even Rome flock to Abélard. The foreign princes recommend to the King of France the students of their dominions. Abélard revolutionises the teaching of dialectics and theology which had gotten stuck in the conservatism of the Church since Charlemagne. Abélard, the dialectician, dethrones the great Anslem of Laon. He is the uncontested, unchallenged professor who is admired by his students. One such admirer of Abélard is the niece of the chanoine Fulbert, the beautiful and brilliant girl, named Héloïse. The chanoine requests Abélard to give private lessons to Héloïse which becomes the cause of his ruin as well as his celebrity. Their romantic liaison becomes a public affair. Abélard is physically assaulted and exiled from Paris, and, the first "femme savante" of Latin Quarter is sent to the convent. Abélard is persecuted. He is accused of heresy. As Abélard recovers mentally and physically, he sets up another centre of learning at Nogent-sur-Seine, and calls his domain, Paraclet. Soon Paraclet becomes the centre of all learning in Europe and the Church feels again threatened. The several thousand students from all over Europe are in search of verity which often comes in conflict with the dogmas of the established Church. In 1136 at the age of 55, Abélard returns to his Paris acclaimed by his disciples and faithful students. The whole of Latin Quarter is surrounded by the admirers of the great Abélard. The immigrant students occupy every house of the area and a whole new quarter is raised to accommodate the growing student population.

Abbé de Clairvaux, the future saint of the Church, denounces Abélard: 'We have in France a monk without regulation, a preacher without solicitations, an abbé without discipline, a serpent who moves around in his cavern ... This persecutor of our beliefs, an outsider, a heretic is surrounded by a crowd of innocent people, he reasons on our beliefs in the streets and the squares, seduces children and women, and signs with his plume the most detested heresies on our most sacred dogmas." His disciples proclaim : "The teaching is an affair of the youth. The students have the right to choose their own masters and they have the right to accept or criticize them. Knowledge is discovered and elaborated progressively, and, none has the monopoly of verity." However, this does not help Abélard, and at the Council of Sens, Abélard is excommunicated and his writings are set to fire in public. Abélard finishes his last days in the monastery of Cluny. His disciples continue the fight. Jean de Salisbury, who is also condemned, declared: "My faith in liberty, my love for verity, these are my crimes." Arnaud de Brescia attacks the despotism of the Church. He crosses the Alps and heads a sedition against the Pope. He dies crucified, and, his ashes are thrown in the Tibre. The Bishop of Paris complains : "These young men have no respect for the hierarchy based on age and experience. These adolescents have the impudence of occupying these "chairs magistrates" they have barely any hair on their chin and they sit proudly in the places of mature men." But the tradition of Abélard continues. And by the beginning of the thirteenth century, the University is recognised by the King as an independent body which, in the following centuries, makes and unmakes kings and popes. Since 1378 two popes claim papal crown. The King of France is for Clement VII, the first Pope of Avignon elected by thirteen dissident French cardinals. England and Germany defend the right of Urbain VI, the Pontiff of Rome. As

the Pope of Avignon is in the pocket of the King of France, the Sorbonne favours the far-away Pontiff of Rome. The death of these two Popes does not solve the dispute. The Roman conclave elects Boniface IX, while the college of the cardinals of Avignon selects Benoit XIII. The University votes against Benoit XIII who threatens to close the University. The King wants an autonomous Church of France so that his nominated cardinals do his bidding, while the University cherishes independence from the King by siding with the Pontiff of Rome. Finally, Benoit XIII excommunicates the whole faculty of theology of Paris and deprives the University of its right to teach. When the Act of Benoit XIII arrives, the King Charles VI is present in the Assembly. The theologians tear away the Bull and the messengers are insulted. As the quarrel between the Popes continues, the University of Paris is able to get a third Pope elected at the Council of Pisa in 1409, where out of 120 electors, 80 belonged to the Sorbonne. The third Pope, Pierre de Condie was an old student of the Latin Quarter. The Italians are furious : these French theologians have a basket full of Popes. They can bring out one whenever they so desire.
At the same time, a professor of Sorbonne, Jean Gerson, fights against the absolute authority of the Pope of Rome. He openly declares that the authority of the Church does not reside in the Pope but in the Council whose duty is to instruct the Pope. Gerson proclaims that the University is the real guardian of the verity of the Church. The University is more than the Kingdom, more than the Christendom. It generates all ecclesiastical and political wisdom. During the earlier years of the fifteenth century, the University of Paris played the political game of balancing of power between the Bourgingnons and the Armagnacs. Gerson teaches that the kings are not sacred; they depend upon the will of the learned. For the youth of the Latin Quarter, it is the signal of revolt. At the time of the judgement of Joan of Arc, the Sorbonnists were caught in their own game. They saw in her the standard bearer of the enemies of the University, the Armagnacs, who in 1411, had proposed to the English that the University be transferred to the province. Joan was nationalist against the English while the Sorbonnists were internationalists against their own King. They wanted their own State within a State.

Within two centuries the Sorbonne became the citadel of conservatism and reaction. State within a State, it abandoned its role of avant-garde in thought and word, and, began to exercise its unlimited power of censure. During the twelfth and the thirteenth centuries, the University of Paris was the dominant intellectual force in all Europe. In the following period, it kept all new ideas away from its holy precincts. François Premier was obliged to open a parallel institution, the Collège Royal, the future Collège de France, in 1530, to combat the rigid attitude of the professors of the Sorbonne. Rabelais said that if he were the King of France, he would burn the den of the Devil that the Sorbonne has turned into.
As some of the professors were receptive to the ideas of Luther, he spoke of the Sorbonne as the most Christian, the mother of all learning, and, in all simplicity and faith, he chose Sorbonne for the arbitration of his quarrel with the Pope. The Tribunal of the Sorbonne deliberated over the famous theses of Luther for ten months, and with unanimity, condemned his ideas as heresy and recommended his excommunication. The same fate awaited the most important French philosopher, René Descartes. In the beginning, there was enthusiasm for him. Descartes even dedicated his Meditations to the venerable institution of higher learning. But the Church got the upper hand, and Louis XIV got Cartesianism excluded from the courses of the Sorbonne. The professors who dared oppose this move were expelled. As a theologian later remarked about this process, the theatre of the Sorbonne where the Bull against Descartes was being discussed was a veritable hell. Fortunately, after the death of the monarch, the rebel professors were reintegrated.
This was seventeenth century, the century of Enlightenment. In the eighteenth century, Turgot could save his skin, for even though one of his theses was on the materialist progress of man, the others spoke of the benefits of Christianity. A year later, Montesquieu's L'esprit des Lois was condemned. So was the case with Buffon"s Histoire Naturelle, Rousseau's Emile was subjected to the same fate. One hundred years after its expulsion, Cartesianism was back in the Sorbonne, and surprisingly, now the Sorbonnists made use of Descartes' supposed spiritualism against the materialism of the encyclopaedists. Diderot could be cited in the Sorbonne only a century later. It is said that it always took a hundred years to enter

the citadel of conservatism of the Sorbonne. Until 1870, the twelve Chair Professors of the Sorbonne were called the "douze Grands Dieux", the Twelve Great Gods.

From the seizure of the Bastille in 1789 to the fall of the guillotine on the head of Louis XVI in 1793, all the representatives of France, the Etats Generaux, participated in the most direct democracy in the world for the first time. The National Assembly was occupied, and, day in and day out, the citizens of France debated on the subjects ranging from the education of children à la Rousseau, the universal religion of Supreme Reason, the reforms in language, art, culture, philosophy, to the daily executions of the traitors to the revolution.

Once the students of 1968 occupied the Sorbonne, they had before them the whole folklore of the French Revolution and of the history of the University of Paris. And, as always, beginning from the Middle Ages to the French Revolution, it was a universal phenomenon. The revolutionaries of all Europe always got together in Paris. The awakened spirits were never bound by the national boundaries. Following the Revolution, the University was reformed, and Reason reigned supreme. However, as the Revolution was betrayed, and Napoleon usurped power, the things changed again. When the students of the Ecole Polytechnique refused to pronounce the ritual sermon of fidelity to the Emperor, he was furious. The next day, Napoleon remarked to Monge, one of the founders of the Ecole : "Your students do not like me." Monge humbly replied : "Sire., it took a lot of hard work to make them republicans, give them time to become imperialists:"

When the old kingdom was restored and Louis XVIII sat on the throne of France, the students and most of the professors continued to adhere to the liberating ideas of the Revolution. The professors in the Faculty of Letters, Guizot, Villemain and Victor Cousin belonged to this University Critique, and they suffered for their views. A professor of Law, Monsieur Bavoux taught in 1819 that the criminal code of the State was favourable to the despotic rule, and there was no liberty to think and act according to one's conscience. His course was suspended, and he was brought to trial. The Faculty of Laws was derecognized. Later when there was trouble in the Faculty of Medicine, twenty-eight teachers were dismissed by Louis XVIII, and, a new constitution was proposed to govern the conduct of the students and the professors. So, what the University Grants Commission is proposing today is not new. The establishment always tried to control the erring students and the professors, but alas, they always failed. The successful revolution of 1830 in France gave back to the University of Paris its lost rights.

The little tale of the University of Paris is a part of the folklore of every French student of the Latin Quarter. Edgar Morin's analysis of the movement of May '68 refers to the revolutionary fête. 3 The ritual barricades of the Latin Quarter followed on May 10-11. The factories were occupied by the young workers beginning May 14. On May 22, the strike was all over France, and, on May 24, even the peasants came out in the streets. On May 30, de Gaulle pronounced his televised address. This period of one month corresponds to the next month of return to normalcy with the two tours of elections when the Gaulists won an absolute majority, and, the left lost heavily. There was no economic crisis, there was no recession, and, there was no such thing as the classical struggle of classes. It has been proposed that it was a crisis of civilization, a crisis nourished by an amalgam of the ideas of Marx, Freud, Sartre and Marcuse, a crisis of Liberty, Ouverture, and Creativity. The students re-lived their rich heritage of revolutions since the twelfth century. They enacted a revolutionary fête nourished by historical and imaginary folklore of the revolutions of yesterdays. It was a realisation of their historic conscience. They enacted a revolutionary theatre where both the cosmic and the historical undercurrents interacted. There was the historical axis of the Sorbonne, and then, there were the contemporary movements represented by Mao, Trotsky, Vietnam, Che, etc., whose portraits were all over the walls of the Sorbonne. It was in a way a prodigious ceremony of the cosmic revolution. May '68 was the movement of the crowds in the streets, and, as it often happened in the days of the French Revolution in 1789, the destinies of the university and the body politic of the country changed in a day. It was a total revolution of culture and liberty. It was the extreme example of popular democracy. The Chinese Cultural Revolution could not be considered as their model as it was not orchestrated by the President in power. The extreme wings of the students and the workers forced their leaders to come out in the streets. The leaders, for once, were led by the followers. As one observer remarked, the leaders ran in front of the shouting workers to maintain the façade of their leadership.

In this system of extremely rigid hierarchy, the first target was obviously the professor and his Cours Magistral. This cours is fundamentally a monologue before a large number of silent students. Pedagogically, its character is global and emanates from the person of the teacher. As such, the professor is a model of identification, a positive hero, who holds and interprets the individual as well as collective verity. At the same time, the professor presents to the students a spectacle of liberty in the absolute sense of the term. In the French educational system since the twelfth century, there has been absolutely no constraint on the syllabus of the professor, and, no control on whatever way he wants to evaluate his students. The system is based on the postulate of responsibility, competence, and the conscience of the professor. There is no statutory obligation. Personally, a professor is considered to be infallible. On the other hand, a student is always placed in the position of guilt. There is no contact between the student and the professor, except first as a silent spectator, and then, at the time of the examination, as the one who is interrogated. The relation between the students and the professor is also regulated by means of the system of the selection of the students for the Grandes Ecoles. Somewhat like our institutes of technology, there are in France, Grandes Ecoles for every branch of knowledge. The competitive examinations, or concours where the places are extremely limited, give access to the kids of the French bourgeoisie to enter the higher echelons of the French social order. The French examinations are always in two parts : écrit (written), and, oral (viva). Every viva is conducted by a number of professors, called the jury. This prospect of facing the jury haunts every French student throughout his life, and, at the same time, gives to a professor, unlimited power. The system as such becomes a system of "repression and negative sanctions." Olivier Burgelin argues that it is an authoritarian system at all levels. It never takes account of the will of the students. The authority emanates from a well-established hierarchy. Secondly, the relations of infantile attitude and guilt play a fundamental role in the alienation leading to anthropological movements within the society. Thirdly, this system constitutes a highly hierarchical society where the relations between different categories are "frozen". At the same time, it results in extreme individualism and compartmentalisation. Fourthly, the university system gives the impression of stability and consensus. The society appears to be a purely external universe. As long as there is no reform of the university, the power it depends upon remains invisible as the transformations or the new acquisitions of professors, credits, faculties, are always by co-option without any standardised regulations whatsoever. It is the "tradition" that regulates the working of the university system.

The traditional consensus began to break in the sixties. The old order could continue only if there was an undeclared understanding. The order had to be interiorised to be maintained intact. Those who dominated derived their authority from those who participated in this game of selections and rose to the privileged class. The hierarchical system depended upon a certain correspondence between the temporal power and the spiritual power.

This correspondence began to change contours as there were changes in the class composition of the students. Traditionally, only the French bourgeoisie participated in this fête of the selections to the Grandes Ecoles. This class had not only accepted this system of evaluation, but its own position in the general social order was based on this system of examinations. With changes in society, with the advent of neo-capitalism, a whole new class of petite bourgeoisie entered this domain. These were the students whose parents had never participated in this system. From a certain point of view, there was a sort of decadence in the general social order. The entry of these new students affected all the traditional bodies of student organisations. There were qualitative changes in the main organisation of the students, the UNEF. This was true also of the communists, Catholics, Protestants, etc. Traditionally, the elders in the PCF, the Communist Party of France, could control the leftist students. This paternalism could no more work in 1968. There was a generation gap in all political and cultural organisations. Another phenomenon in this period was that of the atmosphere of reforms. Several committees had advocated for interdisciplinary approach in the Faculties. For some, the model of the American universities was an ideal. This is where the Jewish intelligentsia plays an important role. Because of their demographic spread, the European Jews generally talk of the American system in Europe and, in the American universities, the European immigrants in general and, the Jews in particular, constantly harp on the excellence of the European intellectual tradition. Even though the American model was, by and large, discarded by all, there was progressive introduction of new disciplines like sociology, linguistics and economics in the Faculties of France. The old classical mandarin system was challenged, and, the French youth asked for substantial participation in the academic and administrative affairs of the University, but this reaction and programming was based primarily on the prevalent tradition of France. The themes of the pedagogy of participation, dialogue, and adaptation were the main topics of discussion. The only way to open this dialogue was a recourse to violence. The movement of 22 March at Nanterre was started by a handful of students. The radical minority spearheaded this contestation. The authorities closed the Faculty of Nanterre and threw the students in the streets. The French students then followed the traditional routine of the barricades in the Latin Quarter. The skirmishes with the police on May 10 and 11 sealed the solidarity of the students. The minority was over-night transformed into a majority. The government in panic withdrew, and, the students occupied the Sorbonne. This was a revolutionary fête with thousands of students discussing the modalities of their programmes and the methods of teaching and learning. Most of the professors cooperated with this venture. The eminent professors, who had until now given only Cours Magistral to the silent students, were engaged actively in a continuous dialogue. The model here was not the Chinese cultural revolution, even though the Red Book of Mao was the best seller in Paris for several weeks in 1967, it was primarily the French Revolution of 1789 that inspired them, and, this is why true to their tradition, almost all professors submitted themselves not only to severe interrogation but also to a meaningful dialogue with the aspirations of the French students. But once the dialogue began, the minority of the radicals had to cede to those who had thought about the fundamental problems of education. The violence achieved its main function however. The old university order disappeared and in its place, the legitimacy of the student power was consecrated.

## IV

It has been remarked by several analysts of the events of May 1968 that the industrial proletariat was not the revolutionary avant-garde of the French society. Jean-Marc Coudray believes that if the students movement touched the revolutionary skies, what brought it down was the attitude of the proletariat, its passivity towards the regime, its inertia, and its indifference to all that is not economic. According to him, in May '68, the most conservative, the most mystified, the most blinded by the lurements of modern bureaucratic capitalism was the working class led by the PCF, the Communist Party of France, and the CGT, its front organization amongst the workers. It was the real victim of the society of consummation. Even when the young workers were on strike, they let themselves be led by the inactive leaders. Waldeck Rochet, the secretary general of the party, called the revolution adventurist, and asked his followers to remain within the framework of "legality". He called the propositions of Geismar, Sauvageot, Rocard, Barjonet, on the seizure of power in May as "irresponsible", even "provocative". For Waldeck Rochet, the torch-bearer of the workers of France, there was only one choice, either act according to the essential demands of the workers and bring about necessary democratic change within the context of "legality", which was the position of the Communist Party, or throw the workers out to struggle for power, i.e. to opt for insurrection, for an armed struggle to overthrow the political power. This, according to him, was the adventurist position of certain ultra-leftist groups.

It may be pointed out here that traditionally the Communist Party of France is composed of industrial workers. The left intellectuals by and large adhere to other groups. The situation in Italy, on the other hand, is quite cohesive. The revolutionary Waldeck Rochet continues his argument as the army and the repressive forces were on the side of the established power (as if they are ever on the other side) and as the immense mass of people were absolutely hostile to such an adventure (he conveniently ignored the ten million workers in the streets of France), it was obvious that to be engaged in such a path was simply to lead the workers to the massacre and the suppression of the working class, and its avant-garde, the Communist Party. In other words, the Communist Party led by its leader Waldeck Rochet was simply scared of the revolution of the youth led by the students of France.

The attitude of the classical proletariat has changed in the modem capitalist society. It accepts hierarchy, whether it is political or of the workers unions. It is passive and stuck in inertia. Modem capitalism has changed the traditional Marxist classification, but unfortunately, it remains as the legacy of earlier years. If the workers had shown even one-tenth of the initiative demonstrated by the students, argues Coudray, the bureaucratic apparatus would have fallen apart. Another argument in favour of the new class is given by Alain Touraine. According to him, the movement of May forced a division between the two layers of society. At the heart of the system of production, the managers are on one side, who are supported by the ever increasing number of bureaucrats, exercising the functions of authority, which constitutes the administrative apparatus of the large private or public organizations. On the other side are those who can contest their technical know how and those who are subjected to this system. In earlier days, there was always a conflict between the technically qualified workers and others, today, the dividing line is between the experts and the bureaucrats, or, as it is often said in industry, between those who belong to a linear organization and those who occupy functional jobs. It is a question of a new sociological formation.

The fact that a large number of workers were on strike should not give us the illusion of this working class. The principal actors in the drama, according to Alain Touraine, are what may be called the professionals: the public or private enterprises, teachers, etc. The new class struggle brings in most direct opposition the techno-bureaucrats and the professionals. According to Touraine, there were in fact three large groups of left forces. First, there were the revolutionary students who were isolated in the beginning. The large majority was hesitant, and, joined the movement when the government closed the University and forced them all together in the streets of Paris. But this force of the left was never properly organized. They were no doubt against the established order and the society, but as they crossed the threshold of political action,

they fell apart.
The second left, of course, was the Communist Party of France. According to the analysis of the party, the objective conditions of France did not allow a revolution. They were ready for the seizure of power, not in the streets but legally, in elections, where, of course, they failed miserably. For once, the Communist Party had absolutely no idea of what was going on in its own country. It was mentally stuck in the mechanism of primitive industry. The continuous Marxist studies, so intensively being conducted in France, did not have any effect on its leaders. The party minimised the May movement to the extreme. It called the students irresponsible and adventurists. It is only when its own comrades deserted the party, and the young workers, without bothering to what the paternalistic elder communists were advising, went on strike and paralysed the entire industrial set-up of France that its leaders began to run before their own cadres to keep the façade of leadership.
The third left was the usual socialists led by François Mitterand, who true to his ambition, immediately declared himself a candidate for the Elysée palace. In fact, the left was literally afraid of this total revolution for which it was not at all prepared. At the election, the communists lost a million of traditional votes. The votes of the socialists were reduced by half. Some commentators of that period believed that the revolution was betrayed by the established left, for they could not take over political power in May '68. If the control of political power is the sole criterion, does it mean that now after a decade, the victory of François Mitterand with the help of the communists has made the revolution successful? Certainly not. The seizure of political power at the helm of a revolutionary movement would have meant the restructuring of the entire university and social order. The present victory is a routine affair, perfectly in tune with the rules of the game of the bourgeois society.
One can draw parallel with the JP movement, even though the exact conditions and the nature of the movements were quite different. The JP movement was betrayed by Messers Desai, Charan Singh, Jagjiwan Ram and co, the old residues of the Congress establishment. On their mental horizon, there was nothing but greed and hunger of political power. They were an integral part of a stinking, corrupt system.

The wave of conservatism continued in France. After the parliamentary elections of 1968 which brought de Gaulle back to power by an overwhelming majority, the French bourgeoisie reigned supreme. When de Gaulle quit the following year, the French electorate voted for George Pompidou, the candidate of the French banking houses. He was followed by Giscard d'Estaing, the representative of French aristocracy. Now we have the so-called left of François Mitterand and the Communist Party which is even more conservative at home and in foreign affairs. Last year when Mitterand expelled nearly forty Russian diplomats on charges of spying, a feat unparalleled even by the Americans, the Communist Party of France, the most pro-Soviet party in Europe did not raise a finger, and continued to stay in the cabinet of Mitterand.

The situation in May '68 was certainly revolutionary, believes André Barjonet. The extraordinary power of ten million striking workers, engineers, technicians, and, hundreds of thousands of students in the streets had brought an unprecedented upheaval. The universities and the factories were occupied by the revolutionaries. There were barricades all over Paris, Lyon, Nantes, Bordeaux and several other cities of France. There was a complete political void. First, the Prime Minister, George Pompidou left for Afghanistan, and on his return, General de Gaulle went to Romania. Towards the end of the month, he left for Baden-Baden in Alsace on a secret mission, not known even to his close associates; the objectives of the visit are still a point of controversy in France. The Communist Party and the Confédération Générale du Travail who had always talked of breaking the monopoly of the Gaullist regime, were caught in panic, and, instead of taking advantage of the objective revolutionary conditions created by this popular movement, denounced the "provocative and adventurous" character of the "insurrectionists". In fact, there was a revolutionary situation created by the initiative of the young students and workers, but there was no revolutionary political party of the masses to take advantage of it. A tract of the PCI, Internationalist Communist Party, held totally responsible the Gaullist regime for the violence which was developing in all the cities of France. "It is the Gaullist power that has taken initiative in the fights and the savage suppression of the 60,000 young workers, students, teachers assembled before the railway station of Lyon. Today, in the struggle which is awakening all France, where Paris,

Lyon, Marseille, Nantes. Bordeaux. Strasbourg rise to face the forces of coercion of a State in the process of decomposition, plebiscitaire referendum is not the answer. The veritable referendum is the general strike. The power is in the streets, and, not in the ballot box. The Marxist-Leninist Communist Party of France declared that there are two sides : the power of the monopolists which unleashes violence on the people, and, on the other, the popular power of the workers, peasants and students who work for the revolution.

"The victory will belong to the people only if there is unity of struggle ... At present, the revisionist leaders of PCF, the Communist Party of France, and its workers wing, the CGT, are spending all their energy to divide the popular forces. They are trying systematically to push the workers against the students. Moreover, they limit their workers struggle to only the domain of petty gains, while the immense mass of workers aspires for socialism. Such manoeuvres have the only objective of serving the dominant ruling class, the monopolist bourgeoisie. The central committee of the Marxist-Leninist Communist Party of France renews its appeal for the constitution of popular committees of action in all quarters, factories, villages, faculties, colleges. Such organizations should spearhead the revolutionary aspirations of the people and organize the necessary action to realise their victory. It is with the overthrow of the power of the monopolists, and, not by a plebiscitaire referendum that the great historical changes of our society can take place." A tract of the Committee of Action reacted thus to the declaration of referendum: to break our movement of ten million workers on strike which threatens to overthrow the Gaullist power, it has ordered re-election of the parliament as the only response to the unsatisfied demands of the workers. In spite of the fact that the established political organizations of the left are playing in the hands of the political power by submitting themselves to the bourgeois legality, the majority of the workers and students have understood that the election will not resolve any problem. The power of the monopolists has taken a step back only because the movement has developed outside the parliament. The parliament is only a tool of the bourgeoisie which makes use of it whenever it needs it. It is not a tool of the workers. For the workers, the only means is a struggle of the masses and the general strike. For the workers and the students, the election is a farce. The bourgeoisie will never lose power in the ballot box. It can be snatched only in the factories and in the streets. The referendum proved that these young revolutionaries were right in declaring the futility of the elections. Whether they could generate a revolution in the streets in May '68 is another question which can never be answered.

The revolution was lost but the revolutionary process continues. There have been several elections since and the bourgeoisie continues to flourish. As the French Revolution of 1789 absorbed a new class of French bourgeoisie in the echelons of the privileged hierarchy, with May '68, France has accepted the aspirations of the emerging new class generated by the growth of neo-capitalism. Violence achieved its limited objective. Dialogue and participation are the key words of every establishment. The University has achieved a certain amount of autonomy. There are more posts of professors. The researchers and young students have considerable role to play in the organization of the university affairs. Of course, this is mostly true of the lower levels of education. The Cours Magistral, however, continues at the Ecoles des Hautes Etudes and the Collège de France. The changes have taken place but they are in the general French tradition. There is no substitute for the selections to the grandes écoles, and, the professors have to work hard to stay in the front line as leaders of thought. The myth of the great professor and the good student continues. The chairs continue and the notions of university departments have been discarded as American, and consequently, anti-national. Some twenty professors of the Collège de France, the living gods of higher education, still have absolute freedom to discourse on whatever they like without any restraint whatsoever of examinations or syllabus. The only control as ever is intellectual. The French society is a prisoner of the ideas of intellectual liberty perpetuated by Abélard, Descartes, Rousseau, Voltaire, Diderot and their followers. This existential shell can never be broken.

The extent of the upheavals of the events of May 68 can be explained only in terms of the nature of the French society which is the most controlled hierarchy in the western world. The French polity and the French University correspond to each other in their function and the vicious circle of its immobility. Monopoly is the first law of this institutionalised system. It does not tolerate even the least competition. This explains the concept of one professor per discipline. This monopoly leads to the Cours Magistral, the obligatory discourse where the audience is captive, and, the refusal of all criticism of authority and influence in the administration of the university. The intellectual style, argues Michel Crozier that is closely related to this model of organization plays a considerable role in reinforcing its foundations. Clarity, coherence, formal rigour, abstract and deductive mode of reasoning, all these very French qualities, are the expressions of the mode of its organization as well as that of its existence. Centralisation requires a uniform and standardised universe. Formalism is necessary for the bureaucratic order. Abstract and deductive reasoning ensures its protection against the external world. The university teaching is based on the notions of the distance between the master and the disciple, and, the great intellectual power of the professor who unfolds the truth. The negative reaction, its consequence and the distance to protect both the teacher and the taught, follow from this system. The Cours Magistral is the symbol of this relation and, at the same time, the expression of the didactic style of intellectual act. It is a vicious circle of passivity and opposition. The mode of relation with the rest of the society is based on the primacy of selections as the primary function of education. Its social mission is to realise with rigour the traditional social hierarchy while pretending to give absolute equality for the most prestigious social professions. The primacy of the function of selection ensures the power of the system which is open and closed at the same time. The mechanism of political power keeps a little door open to all, and, shuts it back as soon as an outsider joins the privileged class. The class apparatus regulates itself. Such a system is absolutely insensitive to any change and the only way to introduce any transformation within it is the way of total crisis. The main crisis of May '68 had to be total and it had to aim at total and complete transformation, for all the elements of French culture were interdependent, and, whether it was a question of the Cours Magistral or of human relations or the content of the cultural message or the system of organisation or the selection of the students, they were all totally integrated in the system, and, could not alter one element without inviting a catastrophy of the entire social order. The French system can be changed only by means of a major crisis. The crisis, however, is always a temporary rupture, it never destroys the system. It is like an entre acte or an interval. As the period of confusion disappears, the old order comes back with the necessary adjustment. In a system of this extreme centralisation and the Cours Magistral, there is absolutely no communication between the one who talks and the other who listens. To break this absolute and total non-communication where silence reigns, one has to restore to anti-discourse and direct democracy of total speech. This process is just the reverse of the Discours Magistral. It is matched by the Anti-discours Magistral. The students occupy the place of the Discours, the Sorbonne, and engage in total parole without any fear of any contradiction. But this violent discourse cannot lead to a dialogue. Once the aggression was committed, the government simply withdrew. The political power never negotiated with the students, it simply accepted all. The problem of general culture was also seen in the same context of French tradition. The Sorbonne remained for centuries the temple of classicism with emphasis on literature, mathematics and philosophy. This general culture became completely inadequate for the modern world, but all those who proposed reforms did not understand the aspirations of the French students and the intellectual layers of the French society. All the propositions called for specialisations. The alternative thus was between the classical formalist culture and extreme specialisation. Both the alternatives were rejected. Professionalism was excluded. The role of the University was the transmission of total culture which keeps abreast of the contemporary movements of thought in the various branches of knowledge. The general culture is no more a useless luxury reserved only for a minority of the aristocrats and few marginal creative artists or writers. It has become an essential means of action in a rational world which can be controlled only through the use of these modes of reasoning. The modern French reformers fascinated by the immediate needs of civilization, argues Crozier, contest the classical French culture without proposing anything in its place. Anglo-saxon specialisation is not the answer. Grandes Ecoles are producing all the professionals, but modern man needs the intellectual tool much more than in old days as the modern world is more complicated, more international with all the intellectual interaction of ideas coming from all branches of knowledge and from different intellectual traditions. The classical culture has to be transformed.

This revolution of total culture and total knowledge with the University as its main source involved a new class of students. It was largely a revolt of the petite-bourgeoisie aspiring to join the ranks of the privileged class just as the new bourgeoisie began the upheavals of 1789. One of the main reasons of the current events in the Punjab is also the rise of a new class. The Sikh peasantry with its newly acquired economic prosperity, through green revolution, through immigrant money, and through smuggling, has upset the political, cultural and educational structures of the Punjabi society. One has only to compare the class composition of all the political parties in the Punjab, the Akalis, the Communists and the Congress to see this transformation. Since the ambitions are great and the generative process is slow, there is violence, but violence and desire are psychic correlates. In France, the contestation had to take place amongst the groups whose entry to all promotions and privileged spheres of culture was blocked.

There is a system of competition in all countries but the severity of this merciless system of concours in France is unparalleled. The students revolution thus had a profound impact on the French society as a whole as the parents of the competitors were equally involved in this struggle. It has been argued that the university revolt was a symptom and a result of the way the youth radically questioned the values of the modern industrialised society, or even modern western civilization as a whole. André Malraux, from his ivory tower of the Ministry of Culture, called it the crisis of civilization. Raymond Aron called it the problem of the isolated provincial French students in the big city of Paris. For him, it was simply a problem of the alienated youth. How nave and simplistic can one be when one reaches the higher levels of establishment! There was also the paternalistic attitude of the leaders of the Communist Party who preferred the nice bourgeois habit of going to the ballot box in clean Sunday suits. When the black Americans burnt Detroit, President Kennedy proposed the installation of swimming pools in the black ghettos to satisfy their frustrations. Marie Antoinette had asked for the distribution of cakes as the demand for bread of the hungry Parisians could not be met. General de Gaulle also talked of the crisis of French boys who put their feet on the tables, and, of the girls who come home late in the evening.

The French youth laughed, but the General won, for the youth had no votes, and the parents took the advice of the General seriously. The crisis of May 68 found in the University, a significance and a function, argues Olivier Burgelin. This does not mean that it did not involve what was around and outside the university. It does not imply even that the ideological models did not have a role to play, but all these conceptual propositions were crystallized only within the framework of the revolutionary activity of the students. The University was not an autonomous entity. It had its external rapports. There could not have been any university revolt without the mental extensions which covered all French intellectual and political history, but all this had to have a centre, a focus. It was provided by the intense intellectual pressure to which the students are subjected every day. The reaction was both violent and deductively logical in the true French tradition. A new scientific culture was proposed in the place of the old order and this is where precisely lies the main significance of the Revolution of May '68.

## REFERENCES

1. Dossiers Clio: Mai 68, Révolution ou pschodram ?. PUF 1973.

2. André Coutin: Huit siècles de violence au Quartier Latin, Paris. 1958, pp. 5-68.

3. J Edgar Morin: Pour une sociologie de la crise, Communication Seuil, 1968.

4. Olivier Burgelin: La naissance du pouvoir étudians, Conununication, Seuil, 1968, pp. 11 -38.

5. George Lanteri -Laura and Michel Tardy: La révolution étudinate,
Conununication Seuil. 1968. pp. 145-47.

6. Jean-Marc Coudray: Mai 1968, Paris, 1968. pp. 116-17.

7. Waldeck Rochet: Les enseignements de mai-juin 1968, Paris, Editions Sociales, 1968, pp. 20-30.

8. Alain Touraine: Le mouvement de mai ou le communisme utopique,
Paris, Seuil, 1968, pp. 29-30.

9. André Barjonet: La révolution trahie de 1968, Paris. Didier. 1968. pp. 15-32.

10. Tract du PCI, Parti communiste internationale. 1968.

11. Tract de parti communiste marxiste léniniste de France. 1968.

12. Tract des comités d'action. 1968.

13. Michel Crozier: Révolution libérale ou révolte petite bourgeoise? Communication. Seuil, 1968, pp. 17-38.

14. Ibid.

15. Raymond Aron: La révolution introuvable, Paris. Fayard, 1968. pp. 42-45.

16. Ibid. 05.

# THE TRIAL OF JOAN OF ARC

## INTRODUCTION

Joan of Arc or Jenne d'Arc, as she is referred to with her French name throughout the English translation of the transcript of the Trial, and as she will be referred to in this essay, was tried at Rouen by the highest ecclesiastic authorities and the doctors of theology of the University of Paris at the behest of the English to whom she was sold by the French traitors.

"There has surely been no more dramatic or horrible trial in history than hers. Sixty of the ablest politicians and academicians, endowed with authority no less impressive because it was largely usurped, were summoned by their military masters to try, under the elaborate forms of law, a girt nineteen years old : an extraordinary girl whose military genius had made her the wonder of Europe, a King-maker, and the archenemy of her judges.

This trial which took place before an English-backed church court in Rouen, France in the first falf of the year 1431 was, in the minds of many people, one of the most significant and moving trials ever conducted in human history. The world had seen nothing like her since the trial of Jesus Christ.

The judges and assessors at Rouen knew as they assembled there that the eyes of Christendom were upon them and that dynasties trembled in the balance. They also were aware that the King of Heavens spoke through His saints. They knew that Jenne had declared that she would raise siege of Orleans and had done so. They knew that she had promised she would have the Dauphin crowned at Reims. She led the Dauphin and his court through English-conquered territory to Reims, subduing Meung, Beaugency, Jargeau and Patay, and had seen him crowned Charles VII, King of France. She had captured the greatest English generals of the time. ..The judges knew that an ecclesiastical examination at Poitiers, conducted by the Archbishop of Reims, then in exile, Cauchon's superior in the Church, had found her good and a true Catholic inspired.

The Trial Record shows us, day by day, how they prosecuted the case, and what their individual decisions were. It is one of the most fascinating narrative in all history...Five copies were made of the official record. Manchon, the notary, wrote three in his own hand : one was given to the Inquisitor, another to the King of England, a third to Pierre Cauchon. These five copies were signed and authenticated by the notaries, Manchon, Boisguillaume and Taquel, and were given the seal of the judges."

Coley Taylor
University of Fordham, New York

# THE TRIAL

(The Trial of Jenne d'Arc was translated into English from the original Latin and French documents by W. P. Barrett, University of Fordham, 1932)

The trial began with the jury constituted of the following ecclesiastic authorities of the church, reverend fathers, lords and masters : Gilles, abbot of Ste. Trinité de Fécamp Pierre, prior of Longueville-Giffard, Jean de Chatillon Jean Beaupère Jacques de Touraine, Nicolas Midi, Jean de Nibat, Jacques Guesdon, Jean Le Fèvre, Maurice du Quesnay, Guillaume Le Boucher, Pierre Houdnec, Pierre Maurice, Richard Prati, and Gerard Feuillet, doctors of sacred theology; Nicolas de Jumièges, Guillaume de Ste. Catheine, and Guillaume de Cormeilles, abbots; Jean Garin, canon, Raoul Roussel, doctors of canon and civil law; William Haiton, Nicolas Couppequesne, Jean Le Maistre, Richard Le Grouchet, Pierre Minier, Jean Oigache, Raoul Le Sauvage; bachelors of theology; Robert Le Barbier, Denis Gastinel, Jean Le Doulx; bachelors of canon and civil law; Nicolas de Venderès, Jean Basset, Jean de La Fontaine, Jean Bruillot, Aubert Morel, Jean Coloombel, Laurent du Busc, and Raoul Anguy; bachelors of of canon law; André Marguerie, Jean Alespeé, Geoffrey du Crotay, and Gilles Deschamps, licentiates in civil law. These were the judges who began to interrogate a peasant girl of nineteen who had apparently disturbed the established order of the King of England and the ecclesiastic domination of Christendom.

The first move was about taking the oath of telling the truth and nothing but the truth but the way it was formulated obviously did not suit Jenne and hence begins the endless polemic. To the deviating questions and the theological traps of the judges, Jenne's replies were highly sophisticated. She was asked "to speak the truth upon those things which are asked her concerning her faith which she knows. She replied that concerning her father and mother and what she had done since she had taken the road to France, she would gladly swear; but concerning the revelations from God, these she had never told or revealed to any one, save only to Charles whom she called King; nor would she reveal them to save her head; for she had them in visions or in secret counsel."

The following day, to the same question, her reply was "you may well ask me such things, that to some I shall answer truly, and to others I shall not. If you were well informed about me, you would wish me out of your hands. I have done nothing except by revelation."

"Again we required her to swear, precisely and absolutely. Then she answered that she would willingly say what she knew but not all. She said also that she came from God, and there is nothing for her to do here, and asked to be sent back to God, from where she came."

"The voice comes from God; I believe I do not tell you everything about it; and I am more afraid of failing the voices by saying what is displeasing to them, than of answering you."

"Then we required her to swear to answer truthfully she should be asked. She replied as before, saying, You ought to be satisfied, for I have sworn enough."

In other words, Jenne would tell the Jury what she wants to and no threat of the judges could force her to deviate from the path she has chosen following the revelations, instructions of the saints, the messengers of God. She would submit only to the Church of God and not to the church on this earth. Slowly and steadily, she is gaining absolute control of herself, spiritually and existentially. In the intellectual gymnastics with the all powerful, all knowledgeable doctors of theology, she is progressing towards the Becoming of the Being of JENNE D'ARC.

To confuse Jenne, the jurists ask all kinds of silly questions. In which garb the saints appear to her? How are they dressed? What is the colour of their habits? Jenne is never taken in. For her, the appearances are holy and sacred visions. There is no question of forms and silhouettes? What the voices tell her is absolute secret, charged with purity and piety, with the knowledge of past, present and future. This knowledge is divine and cosmic. The ecclesiastic authorities can never comprehend this most sacred revelation.

Once the jury even asked her if the saints speak French or English. Of course, French, quick came the answer, for God and the saints are on the side of French. They want the English to leave France and go back to their home in England. God has commanded her to fight the English and throw them out of her homeland. All her victories were God's victories. Very soon, all the English armies will be annihilated and France will be free of the English to the last soldier alive.

And this prophesy came true. Jenne, dead, was more dangerous than alive. Her martyrdom inspired the usual passive French army and within a couple of years, the English fled from the soil of France. The hundred years' war was over in a few years. Obviously, Jenne's spell was all over Christendom. The most experienced generals and the brave soldiers of the English army were defeated by this nineteen years old peasant girl.

With this interlude, let us continue with the Trial.

"Then she was questioned about a certain tree growing near her village. To which she answered that, fairly near Dormrémy, there was a certain tree called the Ladies' Tree, and others called it the fairies' Tree; and nearby is a fountain. And she has heard that people sick of the fever drink of this fountain and seek its water to restore their health; that she has seen herself; but she does not know whether they are cured or not.
She said she has heard that the sick, when they can rise, go to the tree and walk about it. It is a big tree, a beech, from which they get the fair May." (152)

This is excellent anthropology. In these Middle Ages, in the Dark Middle Ages of Europe, such trees are all over. Even in India, even today, in the countryside, there are numerous such legends. It is obvious that when men do not tell the truth or face the truth, the

old trees do their job. In many cultures, the trees, different animals, snakes, birds, fishes, crocodiles are known to foresee the future of all of us. They know the past, present and future of all, the past, present, future that we human beings refuse to confront. As a child, Jenne grows in this legendary atmosphere but she soon overgrows these preliminary signs. She is led to higher visions of the saints and the angels of God. The scope, space and time of her visions is cosmic and she transcends the logic of the ecclesiastic doctors and the military genius of the captains of the armies.
It is interesting that more often than not the accusations of the judges tell more about Jenne than her own answers. Of course, how could she know that these very ordinary things that she has experienced are the most significant for these doctors of theology. They wanted to prove that she believed in evil spirits, in superstitions, in the most backward acts of nature. What they did not realise was that there was more wisdom in nature than in culture, the culture that was infested by injustices, forced conquests of other peoples lands, by the unpardonable inequality of gender and race.

At the age of seventeen when God sent her on a mission to clear all English soldiers of French soil, she put on a male soldier's dress to ride a horse and to wield the sword. This was obviously not acceptable to church and society. God made her woman and she must dress like a woman and perform all the household duties of a woman ordained by God. Jenne refused to listen to this advice of the church. She was commanded to be the Chef of the French army and as such she must wear the dress of a male soldier. There are enough women to do household work. Her destiny is different. She has been chosen by God to deliver her country of the hordes of English who have occupied her homeland, her country, her sacred home.

It must be underlined that in all cultures, the dress code of women, is the most significant sign to keep women in their place. Almost all religions are preoccupied with this fetish. It is through dress that women can be subjugated for ever. In the early years of the fifteenth century Jenne dares the ecclesiastic authorities. She is a soldier, irrespective of being a male or female. She will ride the horse and wield the sword with which she will throw out the English who have been occupying parts of her homeland for almost a century. Now it is their turn to leave. She writes to the King of England :

"King of England, and you Duke of Bedford, calling yourself regent of France, you, William Pole, Count of Suffolk, John Talbot, and you Thomas Lord Scales, calling yourselves lieutenants of the said Duke of Bedford, do right in the King of Heaven's sight. Surrender to the Maid sent hither by God the King of Heaven, the keys of all the good towns you have taken and laid waste in France. She comes in God's name to establish the Blood Royal, ready to make peace if you agree to abandon France and repay what you have taken. And you, archers, comrades in arms, gentle and others, who are before the town of Orleans, retire in God's name to your own country. If you do not, expect to hear tidings from the Maid who will shortly come upon you to your very great hurt. And to you, the King of England, if you do not thus, I am "Chef de guerre"; and whenever I meet your followers in France, I will drive them out, if they will not obey, I will put all to death. I am sent here in God's name, the King of Heaven, to drive you body for body out of all France. If they obey, I will show them mercy. Do not think otherwise; you will not withhold the kingdom of France from God, the King of Kings, Blessed Mary's Son... If you do not believe these tidings from God and the Maid, wherever we find you, we shall strike you and make a great tumult than France has heard for a thousand years...The Maid prays and beseeches not to bring yourself to destruction. If you obey her, you may join her company, where the French shall do the fairest deed ever done for Christendom. Answer, if you desire peace in the city of Orleans; if not, bethink you of your great hurt soon. Written this Tuesday of Holy Week." (175)

Here is a letter presented by the judges to accuse Jenne of a merciless peasant girl, who calls herself, the Chef de Guerre, who is inspired by evil spirits, who is blood thirsty, who cares a little for spilling the blood of humanity.

"The said Jenne, usurping the office of angels, said and affirmed she was from God, even in things tending to violence and to the spilling of human blood, which is absolutely contrary to holiness, and horrible and abominable to all pious minds."... Jenne answers that she first asked for peace, but if peace was not agreed to, she was prepared to fight."

During the Vietnam war some such pious souls asked for peace, to stop war. Jean-Paul Sartre replied, we want peace, but not at any cost. The Vietnamese are not only fighting for the freedom of Vietnam but for the freedom of of all of us, of all humanity. Jenne d'Arc in the fifteenth century was not only fighting for the freedom of France but for all humanity. She refused to be classified as a woman to wear woman's dress and get imprisoned for life in the household work. In those Dark Middle Ages of Europe, she was fighting a war which is still continuing in the twenty-first century all over the world. As Chef de Guerre, she defeated the most professional armies. As a woman, she showed what a woman can do, what no man in France could do at that time.

In the Middle Ages, even church believed that one can hear the voices of God and His saints. The only question was that they were supposed to prove that the so-called voices that Jenne was referring to were in fact the voices of evil spirits, the demons. This could be proved only if the cause was just or unjust. Obviously, for the hired church and the ecclesiastic authorities, the cause of Jenne, to deliver her country of the English, was unjust. Hence her voices could not be the voices of the saints, the messengers of God. The Christian God forbade the spilling of blood and Jenne was bent upon fighting, destruction and devastation. In the run up to this enterprise, the spilling of human blood was a necessary element which had to be condemned if one is a good Christian. As a woman, Jenne was supposed to wear woman's dress, and spend her time in spinning, weaving, doing household work and being a shepherd in the fields of her parents. As a Chef de Guerre, she was dressed as a male soldier, in the company of other male soldiers, fighting and killing. She had brought a curse on the whole womankind. She must be condemned to be burnt at the stake. She knows how to inspire her men. "The said Jenne put a spell on her ring, her standard, on certain pieces of linen or pennons, which used to bear or have her men before her, as did upon the sword she claimed to have found by revelation at St. Catherine de Fierbois, affirming that these objects brought good fortune. She uttered many curses and incantations over them in different places, publicly declaring that with their aid she would do great things and overcome, her enemies, that her men could meet with no defeat in their attack or fighting, or suffer any misfortune, because they bore such pennons." (171)

This is presented as an accusation for her superstitions by the judges. In fact, even if one takes them as true, they do wonders in inspiring her men to fight. After all, we are dealing here with discourse of the middle ages. What else one expects in such circumstances? Even if one takes these charms as superstitious tricks, the fact remains that they worked. The soldiers of Jenne defeated the English at several occasions inspired by these charms, however unchristian they may be, declared by the ecclesiastic authorities. The common French believed in her declarations. She was sent by God. She hears the voices of saints like Catherine who bring to her the messages of God. The angels bring the signs which convince the Dauphin of her divine mission and gives her a large army. It is the same army which had been defeated again and again by the English. Jenne has convinced her soldiers of the divine mission of throwing the English out of French soil. They fight with her, along with her, riding the charger with the sacred sword in hand. The victory is certain. Even in occasional defeat, she wins. Even after her death, after her burning on the stake, the French keep on defeating the English, and within a very short time, they get rid of all English soldiers, body by body, soldier by soldier, as had proclaimed Jenne when she was alive and frightening the entire English establishment.
Let us follow a few more accusations of the venerable ecclesiastic authorities.

"The said accused, not only in the present year, but from the time of her childhood, not only in your diocese and jurisdiction, but also in the neighbouring and other parts of this kingdom, has performed, composed, mingled in and commanded many charms and superstitions; she has been deified and permitted herself to be adored and venerated; she has called up demons and evil spirits, has consulted and frequented them, has had, made, and entered into pacts and treaties with them; and has induced them to do the same or like things, saying, believing, maintaining, affirming, that so to do, to believe in them, to use such charms, divinations and superstitious proceedings was neither a sin nor a forbidden thing; but she has rather assured them that it is lawful, praiseworthy and opportune, enticing into these evil ways and errors many people of different estate and of either sex, in whose heart she imprinted these and like things." (148)

"The accused is fallen into many diverse errors of the worst kind, infected with heretical evil: she has said, uttered, voiced, affirmed, published, graven on the hearts of simple people certain false and lying propositions, infected with heresy and actually heretical, without and contrary to our Catholic faith, against the statues made and approved by the General Councils." (149)

As stated earlier, Jenne's initiation into evil spirits and demonic powers began when she was a child and used to frequent an old tree near her village.

"Near the village of Domrémy stands a certain large tree, commonly called "l'arbre charminé de Bourlemont," and near the tree, there is a fountain. It is said that round about live evil spirits, called fairies, with whom those who practice spells are wont to dance at night, wandering about the tree and the fountain." (151)

"The said Jenne was wont to frequent the fountain and the tree, mostly at night, sometimes during the day; particularly, so as to be alone, at hours when in church the divine office was being celebrated. When dancing she would turn around the tree and the fountain, then would hang on the boughs garlands of different herbs and flowers, made by her own hand, dancing and singing the while, before and after, certain songs and verses and invocations, spells and evil arts." (152)

As a child, Jenne liked the company of the fairies. She danced and sang, alone, and at times with other girls. She knew that these spells had some power, for they cured the sick, and helped children to grow healthy and happy. These may be superstitions or the work of the evil spirits, she did not know. In any case, all of this changed when at the age of thirteen she began to have the visions of the saints who had been sent by God. She was the chosen young girl who was being commissioned by God to deliver her country of the English. She should learn to ride a charger and wield the sword.

"Jenne, when she was about fifteen, of her own will and without the leave of her said father and mother, went to the town of Neufchateau in Lorraine and there for some time served in the house of a woman, an innkeeper named La Rousse, where many young unguarded women stayed, and the lodgers were for the most part soldiers. Thus, dwelling at this inn, she would sometimes stay with said women, sometimes would drive the sheep to the fields, and occasionally lead the horses to drink, or to the meadow, or pasture; and there she learned to ride and became acquainted with the profession of arms." (154)

It may be noted that as a young peasant girl, Jenne had no idea of a war horse, a charger, a sword or a spear. This is the first occasion when she gets some training in the wielding of arms and in riding horses. Since childhood, she has been in the company of fairies and their charms and spells. At the age of seventeen, Jenne is charged with the mission of defeating the large professional armed forces and crowning the reluctant Dauphin. Followed by a few peasant soldiers, she sets out to reach Reims which is well in the English occupied territory. She avoids the big cities, and with help of the village informers, defeating the few scattered English soldiers, she reaches Reims. Now she has to convince the Dauphin that hers was indeed a message sent by God. She showed him the Royal Insignia brought by the angels and somehow was able to convince him of the divine ordination. With the help of the divine sword and the army that was provided by the newly crowned king, she sets out to defeat the English who have been there for several decades. In fact, this civil war was going on for almost a hundred years. That within a couple of years she could defeat the most battle hardened English armies was no less than a miracle. In fact, one of the accusations was that her victories were due to her spells and her sacred sword. By the time she was captured, sold to the English, tried and burnt on the stake, she had almost decimated the English power, for in a few years after her death, martyrdom, the same French soldiers who had never won any battle before the advent of Jenne, now took only a few years to completely wipe out the last vestiges of the English. The dead Jenne proved much more dangerous than the Jenne when she was alive. No wonder, that the most venerable doctors of theology of the University of Paris and the ecclesiastic authorities could not comprehend this highly complex person, called Jenne d'Arc. Even her man-woman fusion in her habit of a male soldier was too much for them. By dressing like a male soldier, she had inadvertently destroyed the whole edifice of the church which was both anthropologically and cosmologically based on this male-female distinction. In fact, all societies and religions are stuck since times immemorial in this physical and conceptual construct. If it is ignored and deliberately transgressed, there is not much left in the metaphysics of our cultures.

"The said Jenne having repeatedly asked permission to hear Mass, was admonished to put off man's dress to return to woman's dress; her judges gave her hope that she would be allowed to hear Mass and receive Communion if she would finally put off man's dress and wear female attire, as befits her sex. She would not agree, and preferred not to take communion and the holy offices; abandon this dress, pretending that so doing she would displease God, so revealing her obstinacy, her stubbornness in evil, her want of charity, her disobedience to the Church, and the scorn she has of the holy sacraments." (164)

"The said Jenne, after her capture, at the castle of Beaurevoir and at Arras, was repeatedly and charitably admonished by noble and eminent persons of both sexes to abandon man's dress and to wear habits decently fitting her sex. This she absolutely refused, and still obstinately persists in her refusal to do, as well as the other duties fitting her sex; in all things she behaves more like a man than a woman." (166)

This is the crux of the problem. "She behaves more like a man than a woman". And that is not acceptable to the Christian Church, and in a way, to all churches. This woman has transcended the male-female distinction. The male dress is the signifying feature, the celestial sign, that guarantees her Being as a pure, brave Being, beyond all cultural and religious bonds. And obviously, it cannot be tolerated. She must be burnt at stake. She would have been, in any culture, in any religion, faced the same fate.

"The said Jenne presumptuously and rashly boasted of knowing the future and having known the past, of discovering things secret or hidden; and this attribute of God she attributes to herself, a simple and unlearned creature." (183)

Yes, this "simple and unlearned creature", that Jenne is supposed to be by the learned doctors of theology, how dare she claim to know anything? Knowledge is the domain of men, of male philosophers, how dare this "mad woman" as she is presented in another accusation, dare speak like a wise man? Once there was a question of negotiating with the English. The newly crowned King Charles was ready to negotiate. Jenne advised him not to indulge in such a treaty with the English. She was sure, nothing would come out of such an enterprise. The English have occupied large tracts of the country. They will never vacate it of their own will.

"The said Jenne, as long as she remained with the said Charles, dissuaded him and his men with all her power from negotiating any treaty with his enemies, continually incited her party to murder and shed human blood, affirming that there could be no peace but by the sword and the lance's point: that it was so ordained of God, since the King's enemies would not otherwise yield what they held of the realm, and therefore to make war on them was to her mind of the greatest benefit to all Christendom." (168)

What was so obvious was considered by the holy judges to be a crime against humanity, for it would lead to the shedding of blood. The occupiers, the imperialists never give up what they have usurped by brute power. What is taken away by the sword has to be taken back by the sword. It is simple logic but when the ecclesiastic authorities, the hired traitors want to sabotage, no body can stop them. Only a Jenne d'Arc can have the courage and lucid determination that whatever be the cost, the sword must be measured with sword. One should not bother about the consequences. God is on the side of the suppressed, the occupied, the downtrodden. Jenne was a highly determined Being, the most resolute Being that there ever was in human history.

“The said Jenne, in and since the time of her youth, has boasted and daily boasts of having had many revelations and visions, and concerning these, in spite of being charitably admonished and lawfully and properly required upon legal oath, she would not and will not swear, further, she refuses to declare them sufficiently by word or sign; but did and still does put off, contradict, and refuse. And when formally
refusing to swear, on many and several occasions, she said and affirmed, in her examination and elsewhere, that she would not discover her visions and revelations, even if her head were cut off or her body were dismembered; that we should not drag from her lips the sign which God showed her, by which she knew she came from God.” (180)

If there was any doubt about her resolution, her determination, her self- assuredness, her absolute existential realisation, this accusation should be enough. One has to be absolutely colour blind, reason and logic blind, not to notice the most resolute Being that there ever was. She was absolutely certain of her visions, her just cause, her divine path that she was treading. She had acquired an existential, and in the meta-language of the fifteenth century, a spiritual equilibrium, balance, rhyme and reason that could not be shaken, could not be destabilised under the harshest possible punishment that awaits her, of which she is well aware, but she has already transcended all that, and that now no power, however overwhelming it may be, earthly, or of the highest possible ecclesiastic authority, can forbid her from her path, and for her, the God's path, that she has chosen once for all.

And finally, the day of judgement.

“Holy Mother Church and the jurisdiction of the said bishop.
And certainly he, with all solemnity and most honourable gravity,

after securing the collaboration of the vicar of the Inquisitor of Heretical Error, conducted this famous trial for the honour of God and the salutary edification of the people. After this woman had been for many days examined by the said judges, they submitted her confessions and statements to the decision of the doctors and masters of the University of Paris and many other learned authorities, and according to their advice they declared this woman to be manifestly superstitious, idolatrous, a prophetess, a caller up of demons, blasphemous towards God and His saints, schismatic and greatly erring from the path of Jesus Christ. Indeed, to purge this miserable sinner of her pernicious crimes and to medicine her soul in the extremity of its frailty, she was for many days repeatedly admonished by charitable exhortations to reject all her errors, to walk in the straight path of truth and to keep herself from the grave dangers which threatened her body and soul.

But the spirit of pride took hold of her mind so that her iron heart could by no means be softened by healthful teaching and salutary counsel. On the contrary, she obstinately boasted that she had done it all at the command of God Himself and the saints who visibly appeared to her; and, which was still worse, that she recognised no earthly judge, would submit to none except God Himself, and the blessed ones of the triumphant land, and spurned the judgement of our Holy Father the Pope, of the Council General and of, all the Church Militant. From which the said judges, seeing the hardness of her heart, summoned this woman before the people, and declared her errors to her in a public sermon, addressing final warning to her." (374)

The judgement was simple and harsh. If she repents and confesses that she was guided by evil spirits, she can spend the rest of her life in prison. If she persists in her word and thought, she will be burnt on stake.

Suddenly Jenne was frightened. The image of being burnt alive was too much to bear. She became again the young peasant girl. She became human, too human. She repented. The judges and the ecclesiastic authorities had broken this most obdurate soldier.

They could not believe their own eyes. How could it happen?
Back in the prison cell, Jenne reflected on all that had happened. Slowly she recovered her composure. Her existential Being again took over. She was again in the company of her saints, the messengers of her God. They comforted her. The next day, she withdrew her repentance, and asserted her Being in a manner that even the venerable doctors of the University of Paris had not seen.

She was duly burnt on the stake on May 30, 1431.

As for the English, she was more dangerous dead than alive. Her martyrdom surcharged the passive French soldiers. They won victory after victory and within a very short time, they completely wiped out the entire English occupation from the soil of France.

A few years later, the French King, now the victorious King of all France, ordered the retrial. Meanwhile, the Chief Inquisitor had died but there were several judges and witnesses alive who duly scrutinised every paper and declared her innocent of all charges.

## MEDIATION

Jenne d'Arc in the sublime beatitude of Heaven had the last smile !

Her armies had annihilated the last vestiges of the English presence on French soil. The two trials had cancelled each other. The most highly competent ecclesiastic authorities in canon law and theology had no place to hide.
In the cosmic rhythm and reason of Heaven, Jenne reflected upon the human condition, the condition replete with betrayals and empathy, with falsehood and injustice, with absolute ruthlessness of brute imperial power, with the venerable doctors of the Catholic Church being sold for a piece of bread.

What can one say about both the inquisitions? In a way, both were farce. The one, composed of sixty judges, the henchmen of the

Catholic Church, the other decided by another King, now in absolute power. The extremely elaborate Inquisition actually established Jenne as the most knowledgable dialectician.
All through the Trial, she demonstrated her brilliance, in arguing, in saying what she wanted to say, in not saying what she did not want to say. No threat, no threat of stake could break her resolve. She withstood the most elaborate and the most complex Trial that was ever held in the Western world, in all Christendom. It proved nothing. In fact, it was never a question of Right or Wrong. The questions were metaphysical. How could they be solved in a human, empirical court? Jenne had transcended the wrongs and rights of this world. She kept on reminding her judges that she could not be subjected to the court of the Catholic Church, she will submit herself only to the Court of God. She believed only in the Church of God. So the whole exercise was futile. If there was reason, it was transcendental, if there was justice, it was transcendental, if there was truth, it was transcendental. How could the Catholic Court deal with absolute transcendental realm? Jenne had transcended both Right and Wrong. This transcendence, this going beyond all possible logic and reason could not possibly be handled by ordinary human beings, however pedantic they might have been.

The history of the University of Paris has had a very complex career. At times, it followed logic and reason. At others, the faculty was highly conservative. When Descartes insisted that the existence of being depended upon his thinking, the ecclesiastic authorities, the doctors of theology were shocked; human existence no more depended on their God. They banned the writings of Descartes for almost a hundred years. Descartes' philosophical ideas were being discussed in almost all European universities except in Paris. History repeats itself. Now the same university, after the 1968 students' revolution, is named, University of René Descartes. Our universities today are going through the same dilemmas.
And after almost five hundred years, in 1920, the Pope declares Jenne d'Arc as a saint of the Catholic Church. The legend has it that an English soldier could not stand Jenne's burning on stake, and said that today they had burnt a saint. Another commentator remarks that what was obvious to the whole humanity all these centuries, dawned on the Catholic Church after such a long time.

Even during her nineteen years on this earth, Jenne had transcended herself.

By the time of her burning on the stake, she had become an Idea, an Image, a Sign which could not be classified by normal human standards. The Inquisition burnt her body, but it could never burn the Idea, the Image, the Sign.
Even her dress of a male soldier was very ambiguous. Of course, she was a woman. She knew it. The judges knew it. She had transformed herself into the figure of a male soldier to fight with them,to inspire them. The soldiers knew that she was a woman, but not just any woman, a woman transformed into a goddess. She was the messenger of God, her human form was only an illusion. This man-woman Being was obviously an enigma which could not be solved by human logic. Jenne had transcended her condition of womanhood but only transcended. Of and on, she relapsed into her real empirical self and the doubt continued to persist throughout her life. Her grit, her resolve came from her womanhood, her actions in this world were more manly than womanly. The judges kept on saying, she behaves more like a man than a woman, for if she were a woman, they knew how to handle her. The canon law had clearly stated how a woman should behave. And if she were a man, then also there were clear outlines, how to deal with him. But what to do with this woman-man being who cannot be classified with normal standards of theology.

How did it all happen? At thirteen, she began to hear the voices of the saints, the female saints, God sent only the female saints to talk to her, to give her the message of God, who was probably a male. She was supposed to fight the entrenched English armies. But she had never seen a charger, never held a sword. At fifteen, she had the first occasion to ride a horse but certainly not like the ones the soldiers exercise with. At this time, she also had some practice with the sword but how much that could it be without actual warfare? She had never discussed any doctrine of faith with a doctor of theology?

At seventeen, it was all there. God had told her to go to the Dauphin and crown him the king of France. It was a long journey, the path was infested with the English soldiers all over. Somehow her spells worked. With the help of a few ordinary soldiers, she pierced through the vast hinterland to reach the Dauphin. She was able to convince him of the sacred mission that God had ordained. She had to show him the sacred Sign that the angels had brought. Miracle of miracles, Dauphin was convinced, gave her his passive army, with help of which in a short period of two years, she did what the soldiers of yonder days could not do for almost a century.
Once captured, the Trial of the century, of the century of the Dark Middle Ages, begins.

And what a trial ! The simple, unlearned creature, the mad woman, the superstitious peasant girl as she was called again and again, defeated, in the art of argument and logic, the most venerable doctors of theology. The two trials, the first that condemned her and the second that exonerated her from all sins, proved nothing but the comical farce of the Catholic Church. The authorities asked her again and again to tell the truth. But which truth? Jenne knew the Truth, the Transcendental Truth with which the ecclesiastic authorities were not concerned. And, Jenne had nothing to do with the truth of the Catholic Church which was historically constituted within and for a specific space and time.
It was the historical truth. Jenne's truth had transcended all these parameters, all these paradigms which were foreign to the ears of the doctors of the University of Paris.
They were talking about the charms and spells of Jenne on ordinary folks. In fact, they were themselves under the spell of Jenne. Otherwise, what was the need of such an elaborate Trial and the engagement of sixty plus jurists to be able to condemn a simple village girl?
The English were so worried that this simple girl, this magician may not fly away that she had to be kept always, awake or in sleep, in chains with a huge number of guards to keep her in their hold in prison.
The jurists, turn by turn, kept on asking the same stupid questions. Jenne must have been amused at their ignorance and their naïvety. It seems, it is during the trial that she realised her strength. It is

during this farcical trial that she slowly acquired a being of which she herself was not aware of. From a simple “unlearned creature” she acquired the status of a highly sophisticated logician. Even her dress of a male soldier which in the beginning was probably worn to suit the physical hardship of warfare, became a highly metaphysical issue with constant and rigorous investigation into the purpose and theological complexity of this garb.

In a way, every thing Jenne does is extraordinary and must be taken note of. For the doctors of theology, every act of Jenne is surcharged with metaphysical overtones. The doctors of the Catholic Church must spend hours in their libraries to investigate her, to find errors in her faith. The Catholic Church was shattered. Already there were three popes vying for the throne of Rome. Very soon, every country in Europe had its own sect, its own religion. No wonder, she was heralded as the first ”protestant”. It is also proved by the extreme importance this trial was given that every day the minutes were recorded and approved by the jurists. The first copy was in French, it was translated into Latin, in only five copies, three of them are still kept in the most famous libraries. The English translation by the Jesuits is even more painstaking. It compared, word by word, French and Latin versions, so that Jenne may not question its veracity even when is in heaven.

The whole chaos and confusion was about all what had happened. How could a mad woman, a simple, unlearned creature, a peasant ignorant girl, a witch and a sorceress, all these and more such appellations that the jurists used for her, could achieve what she had achieved. With hardly any regular army, she kept on registering one victory after another. The army that Charles gave her was worthless, the only record it had was that of a series of defeats. She had no money to pay the soldiers. There were no arms. She had never led a group of soldiers, how could she lead a conquering army. With a band of a few soldiers, she was victorious all over. The villages she delivered from the English welcomed the soldiers of the saints, fed them, gave them whatever they had, arms and clothes. And so the small band of soldiers was transformed into a conquering army that could defeat the best trained, well disciplined English army with a hierarchy of captains. The soldiers of Jenne decimated this invincible English army that had tasted nothing but victory for years, for decades. It was obvious that it could be only due to the spell of evil spirits, the demonic powers. Hence, Jenne must be tried by an ecclesiastic jury and not by a military tribunal.

As far as Jenne was concerned, she learnt every thing by simple practice, praxis, as we will call it today. If you want to swim, you just jump in water. Jenne learnt to ride chargers by just riding them. She led the band of soldiers by just leading them and slowly and slowly, the number of the fighters grew without giving the impression of some sudden happening. The only thing Jenne was certain was that she was obeying the holy saints, the messengers of God. So to God only she was answerable. The English and the Church never understood it. For them, all her actions were miracles, inspired by the evil spirits, by the Satan himself. This paradox could be resolved only by the tribunal of the most learned doctors of theology of the University of Paris. So such an elaborate Trial was enacted, a spectacle never seen since the Trial of Jesus Christ. The greatest metaphysicians of Christendom began to interrogate the simple nineteen years old peasant girl. In the beginning, she did not understand what was being asked of her. Why the jurists kept on asking to swear by telling the truth? Which truth? She told them she will tell every thing that concerns the trial. She thought, she was fighting, she was captured, it was all about her military campaign. No, the jurists want to know what the spirits, the evil spirits tell her.

For Jenne, it had nothing to do with their trial. Her communion with the saints was her personal affair. It has been going on for years, since she was only thirteen. This communion was sacred and very intimate. It was pleasant, ecstatic, blissful, sublime, nothing to do with the affairs of an ordinary trial with all the bishops hanging around. It was a big spectacle. She enjoyed it, after all, she was a young innocent girl who still liked to dance and sing as she used to do as a child around the old sacred tree of her village.

No, it was a very serious affair, so thought the jurists. She must answer all questions, she must tell the truth, the truth as judged to be true by the jurists. Jenne innocently said: nothing doing, she will tell what she is allowed to tell by her saints. As far as she is concerned, there is but one church, the Church of God and only that Holy Church of God can judge her. She was a resolute, stubborn being, she will tell what she is allowed by her saints, and no power, no punishment can alter her resolve. Her head may be cut, she may be dismembered, her lips shall not reveal the mysteries of her cosmic vision!

Jenne was no ordinary girl even if she did not think so. She was wearing the male dress, she had cut her hair short, five hundred years before it became fashionable with the avant-garde European girls, and of course, with the revolutionary girls of JNU with kurta and jeans. She was riding a horse, wielding a sword as young soldiers do. Of course, she was a girl. She was proud of being one but she did not think that girls are born only to wear clumsy women's dresses or be involved in household work, spinning, weaving, milking cows and taking out the sheep in the fields of their parents. She was not against such work but she thought there were enough girls to do that. She would do what she liked. It was normal for her that every girl should be allowed to do and wear what she likes. What is wrong with it? It is more funny. It makes you more active. With this dress and short hair, one is not stuck just in the company of old mummies. This garb enables you go to discover the world around.

Very simple innocent thought of a girl child !

If there ever was an emancipated girl, it was Jenne, Joan !

But the ecclesiastic authorities did not think so. It was a very serious affair. This woman-man being was very ambiguous. It had transgressed all religious and cultural conventions. It was a very serious metaphysical enigma. She had crowned the reluctant Dauphin. She had led the armies which subdued the most professional soldiers of the English. She followed no conventions, no rules, no laws of Catholic Church. How could she be tolerated in Christendom? She must be stopped, right now. She must be burnt on the stake.

And so they did !